Reviews for *Marriage And The Love Myth*:

"For anyone who is looking to strengthen their existing marriage or create a healthy, strong long lasting marriage, this book is for you! It's refreshing, captivating and life-changing in the most positive ways. Highly recommended."

—Peggy McColl - A New York Best-Selling Author

Marriage and love myth written by Sukhjiwan Singh is an excellent piece of work. This book details how troubled marriages can be saved and strengthened. Each part focuses on different dynamics and complexities of relationships and marriage and is explainedvery nicely with appropriate materials and real life examples. Author beautifullyillustrates down to each principals that can keep marriage grounded in face of variouschallenges couples face over the years. Today when over half the marriages conceived inlove end up in divorce, this piece of work encourages to resolve differences,disagreements and issues to make your marriage successful. It gives you practical toolsto solve individual difficulties and nurture your marriage. This book inspires andenergizes you to turn broken love into 'happily ever after'. Reading this book changedmy concept of marriage for better. I feel this is a much needed guide map for today'syoung people when over half the marriages don't survive past a few years. I highlyrecommend reading this book whether you are already married, about to get married or ina serious relationship. Learning from this book will keep your marriage and family on track of happiness, harmony and love.

—Dr. Harkewal Sekhon

This excellent book provides an insightful look at the importance of marriage and the dangers of divorce. After the wedding bells fall silent, keeping a marriage healthy and strong requires hard work, empathy, and flexibility. Perhaps most importantly, marital success requires a realistic appreciation of what a lifetime commitment truly entails. Romance is important, but the best marriages transcend the romantic and are based on something more profound. "Marriage and the Love Myth" is a practical, commonsense guide to finding and keeping the right partner for a lifetime. All those contemplating marriage, or already discovering its rewards and challenges, should read this book.

—Michael Bishop - An Independent Book Reviewer

It is an easy read in a simple language, so simple that it directly goes to your mind and makes you ponder about yourself and your immediate relationships. From the title of the book it appears that it is for married couples or people in committed relationships, and it was meant to be so but as you go along you find that it is a handbook that can help you in everyday life in all your relationships. Ms. Singh understands the role of ego in creating problems in relationships; and she gives easy steps to handle the situations. She makes you aware how to get away with 'ego' and that it should not stand in the way of having a healthy married life with a strong foundation. She tells us how small acts of kindness, mercies, and gratitudes can keep us together. We all understand that sometimes it is really hard to dismantle our belief system but by following the simple steps given in this book we can change ourselves and redefine ourselves. She has introduced us to real couples and their problems; and by reading these social stories and imagining in their shoes you can really learn how to solve problems.

—Gulshan Dyal - Author of 4 Books

Ms. Singh's insightful study into marriage from choosing a compatible partner to how to get back on track if your marriage derails is an excellent resource on building stronger marriages. It is a very engrossing easy to read book with real life solutions to challenges often faced by couples today. Ms. Singh believes that making marriage successful is a conscious choice. She offers specific approaches to issues facing a married couple and helps to heal a strained relationship. It practically leads couples to enjoy a deeper level of peace and harmony with each other. I have enjoyed this book thoroughly and gained a lot from it. I have shared this book with many friends and family members. I have also sent this book to overseas friends.

—Prabhdip Sekhon PhD. RDN. LD.

MARRIAGE AND THE LOVE MYTH

FROM TURBULENCE TO MARITAL BLISS

SUKHJIWAN SINGH

authorHOUSE®

AuthorHouse™
1663 Liberty Drive
Bloomington, IN 47403
www.authorhouse.com
Phone: 833-262-8899

Published by AuthorHouse 03/31/2021

ISBN: 978-1-6655-1698-3 (sc)
ISBN: 978-1-6655-1697-6 (e)

Dedicated to my children and the youth of all times

You were the sole reason that I was pre-occupied all these years with the subject of marrying right the first time around. I'm truly humbled by your choices of life partners and launch of your careers.

You just have to stay grounded in the principles that have propelled you thus far and on to a beautiful journey. I hope to see you blossom in marital bliss.

And to the **youth**—present and future generations; go forth and take charge—rooted in family values. You can rectify the confusion in the human race of our times by choosing the right course for. The making of a strong family needs you to prepare, learn to bear and weather the terrain of married life.

My son Lally is married to Rukhsanah, with two children—Naeema and Zain.

My younger son Rajan is married to Kirat, also with two children—Gray and Summer.

Thus far, both families are showing all the signs of coming into strong and successful family-units—never wavering in the face of circumstances—fully grounded in their respective roles.

CONTENTS

Foreword..xi
Acknowledgements...xiii
Preface xv

Part One
The Puzzle

Chapter 1   Understanding the Puzzle 1
Chapter 2   The Fundamentals 5
Chapter 3   Are You Compatible? 11
Chapter 4   Are You Sure? 15
Chapter 5   Is Divorce the Only Option?.........................17
Chapter 6   Why Do Marriages Fail?...............................33

Part Two
Finding a Compatible Mate—The Process

Chapter 7   Know Yourself...43
Chapter 8   Self-Analysis 47
Chapter 9   Envision Your Future...................................65
Chapter 10 Find a Compatible Partner.............................67

Part Three
The Marriage Code

Chapter 11   Create a "Mission-in-Marriage" Statement 81

Chapter 12   Principle One: Love and Respect Each Other
Unconditionally 91

Chapter 13   Principle Two: Don't be a Hard-Liner 99

Chapter 14   Principle Three: Compromise Is a Virtue 101

Chapter 15   Principle Four: Don't Try to Change One Another 107

Chapter 16   Principle Five: Don't Compete with Each Other 115

Chapter 17   Principle Six: Understand Your Partner's Perspective .. 119

Chapter 18   Principle Seven: Never Give Up on Negotiation 127

Part Four
Getting Back on Track

Chapter 19   Keeping a Balance 135

Chapter 20   Assumptions and Misunderstandings 139

Chapter 21   Surviving Anger and Disagreements 145

Chapter 22   Diffusing Power Struggles 151

Chapter 23   Surviving Financial Challenges 155

Chapter 24   Surviving Extramarital Affairs 157

Chapter 25   Working through Sexual Problems 165

Chapter 26   Surviving Illness or Death of a Loved One 169

Chapter 27   Last But Not Least 175

FOREWORD

When my wife, Sukhjiwan, first announced to me that she was going to write a book about marital issues, I could see that it was in the works for a number of years. No matter what issues are in discussions among us around the dining table or our bedroom, her arguments always suggest positive solutions.

Engaged in real estate sales, Sukhjiwan has come in contact with all kinds of cultures and ethnicities spanning over the last 25 years. She has a natural talent at building instant relationships. She not only sold houses, but also learned about family values prevalent in different cultures. Her clients instantly begin to confide in her about their interpersonal problems. In fact, she would prefer to counsel a divorcing couple to stay together rather than listing their house for sale.

We started our life's journey from a culture that believed in arranged marriages, and where pre-marital sex was practically nonexistent. We immigrated to United States in late 1979 and walked into a free society with no boundaries. In the United States, we are witnessing new history made by legislations in favor of same sex marriages, but Indian immigrants settled in western culture still practice "honor killings," though sparingly and mostly in some pockets of deeply ethnic settlements. I cannot help but think of the stark contrast between the two cultures- an uncanny transformation! It was our crystal clear belief system that kept us grounded in a successful marriage.

I don't know if other people's problems seek her or she seeks them, but she is always contemplating and discussing people's problems; and I am invited to participate. She became a volunteer with Victim's Assistance

Network for a while; that experience expanded her understanding of real life situations in family relationships among all cultures.

Our marriage, even though was not a typical arranged marriage, we still faced common struggles in our married journey. We made mistakes, we learned a lot and tried to stay focused on creating an environment of nurturing relationships, we have made it thus far—joyfully.

I can assure readers that they are safe using this common sense guide filled with astounding wisdom. Sukhjiwan has walked the talk and I have been fortunate to be walking alongside her for thirty three years.

Happy Reading!

Sincerely,
Malkiat

ACKNOWLEDGEMENTS

I am deeply indebted to my loving husband—Malkiat, for allowing me the freedom to talk about our life so openly. I could not complete this book without sharing my personal experiences in marriage that shaped my thought process, and made me confident enough to share what I know.

In part three of the book, I have written about the "code of marriage," which is deeply rooted in principles. Those principles are not a new invention on my part. Those concepts have been around for hundreds of years. I have attempted to apply those profound principles to the framework of marriage.

The writings of thought leaders like Dr. Wayne Dyer, Jack Canfield, Dr. Deepak Chopra, and Dr. Stephen R. Covey in the field of self-improvement consciousness have lighted my path to stay grounded in principles. Oprah, through her talk show, and Marcia Wieder, through her book *Make Your Dreams Come True*, have ignited the passion in me to embark on my dream to share my two cents through this book.

I'm especially indebted to *The 7 Habits of Highly Effective People* by Stephen R. Covey — It was a gift given to my husband on his fiftieth birthday by our dear friend, Dr. Salvinder Hundal. I read the book, and re-read it. It turned on a light bulb in my mind. I began to see my life through a different prism. I saw a behavioral change in me. I stopped being angry. Whenever I was disappointed by something or someone—in my home, business or social world—my mind started to shift from getting into angry mode to search mode for the "root cause" and "damage control." Since September 1999, I have been continuing on this journey of self-directed transformation.

It has changed my perception on some very fundamental issues concerning marital relationships. I'm happier and profoundly peaceful. I believe that if I can alter my perception for a positive change; anyone can do it.

When I started to write this book, I came across Iris Krasnow's book *Surrendering to Marriage*. I was deeply reassured to know that Iris's findings on marriage and relationships were similar to my belief system. Iris Krasnow is a journalist. She interviewed a wide spectrum of people to write her book. In this book, I wrote stories of folks that I personally know, people that I have interacted with in the social or business world over the last thirty years. Names in the stories have been altered, but the stories are real to the core.

PREFACE

Taking on a subject like marriage with all its challenges and to offer solutions and draft a step-by-step formula was not something I thought about, but the end product finished along those lines. As our two sons were finishing college and coming of age to be married, my mind pondered the many facets of married life. I was happy and I was worried. The divorce rate in this country was the source of my worry.

Then my mind had a flashback to our children's friends who came from steady households, and those who came from single-parent families. I watched those kids for15 years. The kids that came from happy families where they had support from both mom and dad under one roof, fared very well with no emotional set-backs. They completed their education and moved on to the next phases in life. The other group, I noticed had stumbling blocks. Some dropped out of school. Some suffered from "trust" issues. Some could not finish college due to financial burdens. The difference was crystal clear and startling.

Going through my real estate career, I pondered the lives of couples in bad marriages—divorced and single parents—and people in functional marriages. I started to draw some serious conclusions.

This led me to analyze my own marriage; I had the taste of some sweet and some bittersweet memories. I am married to the love of my life, Malkiat. We just celebrated our thirty-third wedding anniversary in September. Was our marriage rock-solid at all times? No, it was very fragile at many times—so fragile that one of us could have walked out any time.

Early on, as our "assumed" concepts of each other confronted us in the face, it was scary. In my case, it was my "unsubstantiated" expectations of my husband, his family, and our interpersonal relationship. My expectations brought me misery. I wanted to change him and expected his family to fit in my mental frame-work that I had learned to-be-right. But thank God, my husband was more level-headed. He accepted me for who I was. He never said much. I read too much into his silence, and came to unfair conclusions. You see, that is the problem with men. They don't communicate the way women want them to. I read an interesting book *Men Are from Mars, Women Are from Venice* by John Gray. Now I know that men and women are wired differently. I wish I had this knowledge way back then; it could have saved me a lot of heartaches.

What kept us going was the faith that we loved each other, and our rock-solid commitment to our marriage. Despite all challenges and disappointments, we stuck it out. I am happy that we did. With every challenge we experienced, new expectations forged out of renewed realities. It promoted hope, and strengthened our commitments. As a result, we have been able to give our children a rock-solid family.

My husband and I both grew up in Punjab state, in the northern part of India. Coming from middle-class families, we both had strong belief systems. We are very different from each other; Malkiat is a physicist, and I love literature. Coming from similar backgrounds, same religion, and being in love—we thought our marital journey would be very romantic—easy and uncomplicated. We were so wrong!

We immigrated to the United States of America in 1979 and settled in suburban northern Virginia. Our older son, Lally, was only five months old, and our younger son, Rajan, was born here a year later. Nonetheless, we became part and parcel of American mainstream suburban culture, and thus a mixture of Eastern and Western value systems.

The broken family system has damaged the fabric of our contemporary social order of Western society. The turmoil and misery in our society is a clear reflection of it. However, it can be salvaged. I am looking at the bull's-eye.

Here is my belief:

When you set out to achieve a goal in life, you chalk out a brilliant plan. Then you work your plan. You tweak your plan on an as-needed basis. Then you end up being whatever you chose to be—be it a career path, academia, or a spiritual journey. Marriage is no different. If you consciously approach marriage with unshakable commitment, having faith in your love and confidence in your vision, then you are bound to make it a success. The formula is very simple.

1. Understand the importance of finding a compatible partner— the first time around. So know "yourself "as you are now, and know your "forging personality". Pick a partner who emulates your vision of a journey together. Life will throw many challenges at you, and that will confuse your concept of love from time to time. Stay committed to your dream of confronting challenges together and having a mutually enjoyable journey—the best it can be.

2. Understand the importance of finding a compatible partner the first time around. So know yourself and know your own forging personality and pick a partner who emulates your vision of a journey together.

3. Lead a life that is rooted in principles and values. I call it—The Marriage Code.

4. To err is human. If you get off track, get back on. Never give up; it is never too late.

We all go through life just like that, one foot in front of the other at a time. If you keep your nose to the grindstone, you will have a happy, enjoyable journey.

Marriage is a commitment for life (or at least, it's meant to be). It impacts people on generational levels. Whereas a strong successful marriage serves as an anchor to the children and their future generations, providing them a laser-focused guidance through highs and lows of life; Failed marriages, on the other hand impact the children so badly that they feel uprooted—their souls bruised—their anchor disconnected. Family is the backbone of any society. A strong-family-culture strengthens the fabric of a society. High divorce rate, juvenile crime, and homelessness in our country stand out as the direct results of a weakened family structure.

How dare we take it so lightly!

PART ONE

THE PUZZLE

Why well intended marriages—conceived in love and trust fall flat; and end up in divorce courts? Why people in love—can't stand the sight of the very person after tying the knot – (they once loved so profusely)? What changes so dramatically that couples feel forced to walk out on each other, and their children—bruising their souls forever.

Is the feeling of love so shallow?

There is only one answer; it lies in the paradigm.

CHAPTER ONE

UNDERSTANDING THE PUZZLE

Marriage is a journey through sweet love and delicious pain packed in with triumphs and disappointments; joys of birth and sufferings of sickness and death; spans of profound happiness and emotional setbacks; financial challenges and failed expectations.

It is also called *life*. Life's events happen whether you are single or married. The good thing about being married is that you do not have to endure life alone. With a strong partnership, you take it with a certain confidence, zeal, and exuberance; life's journey becomes more bearable and enjoyable if you allow it to be.

Most of us know the fairy tale where the prince rescues the damsel in distress and they ride off into the sunset to a place called "Happily Ever After." Many of us think, in some way, that there is truth to this insipid tale. In our modern world, both men and women attempt to rescue, just as both men and women can be a "damsel" in distress. Happily Ever After has a little known subtitle: "Just as long as you work your butt off and are not trying to save anybody or hope to be rescued from yourself." If getting married has anything to do with living out a fairy tale, you may want to reevaluate your decision to be married.

Marriage is one of the most important decision one can make in life. We do so much preparation to

launch a career or a business; truly, what do we do to prepare for marriage? Sadly, nothing much!

Most of us don't know what to expect in the great journey of marriage, and who to turn to when challenges threaten to shatter the lives of its' vulnerable players.

Love alone cannot carry the burden of married life. The warm and fuzzy feeling of being "in love" wears off very quickly as life begins to happen. Once we set out in the role of husband and wife, somehow our expectations of each other, the expectations of our parents or in-laws, and the expectations of friends and family simply take a new form that did not exist before. If you are not ready for this complex role that you are now expected to play, you will find yourself in utter bewilderment.

The only way to a successful and happy marriage is to have realistic expectations of being married and know how to navigate through challenging times.

The tools that will carry you through are love, trust, and an unshakable commitment to stick together through thick and thin.

Many people rush into marriage before they really know what they are getting into. You need time to really get to know the other person. When people first meet and while they are in a dating relationship, they always put their best selves forward and try to hide the aspects of themselves that they think the other person will not accept.

People with unresolved childhood issues bring those into the marriage whether they are aware of it or not, and the issues will play out in the marriage. These problems can eventually be resolved through hard work, but only if both partners are willing to do the work. Often one partner will decide that they didn't get what they bargained for and will leave.

You and your partner need time to discover whether you are compatible. For example, if couples do not agree on how to spend money, whether or not to have children and how they should be raised if they do have children, matters of faith, and what constitutes a healthy sex life, then there could be serious problems in the relationship. Problems can be resolved, of course, but sometimes couples find that there are so many differences that marriage would be a big mistake.

Individuals need to find other means of fulfillment in their lives so that the marriage partner is not seen as the person's savior—marriage should be viewed as being more about giving than receiving. An attitude of "what's in it for me?" will always bring disappointment. Everyone enters into a marriage with expectations about how the marriage will satisfy his or her needs. Problems arise when these expectations go unmet and feelings of disappointment start to seep into the emotional connection between the couple. Many times this is due to one partner expecting the emotional connection to intensify and the other expecting things to stay as they have been. Therefore, it is very important that you talk openly with your partner about what you expect from the relationship—emotionally, financially, and physically—and how you view your future together playing out. Failure to do so may lead the two of you down a bitter path culminating in divorce. Well-functioning relationships are able to survive difficult times and grow as the environment around them changes. All couples experience situations that test their commitment to each other and their compatibility. When you first start dating, it's like summer—peaceful, calm, exciting, and warm. Then winter comes and things often get harder. No longer is one focusing on being on his or her best behavior, and one's "baggage" surfaces. If you haven't experienced all four seasons of your partner-to-be, maybe you should push back the wedding date. If you have, what did you learn about yourself and your partner?

When asked why one is getting married, a common answer is "because I've fallen in love." The wise person knows that with love comes pain. Within every successful relationship, there exists a healthy level of emotional pain that a couple uses to further develop their relationship. Part of making a relationship stand the test of time is to agree to work together to solve problems. Learning how to avoid hurting each other will lessen the chances that someone will stumble and fall, causing both to suffer.

The relationship that our parents had affects us more than most of us want to admit. It is from their teachings and behaviors that we learned about how partners are—and are not—supposed to treat each other. If they were, and still are, great role models, ask them to tell you everything that they have learned about marriage. If they weren't, still ask, but also seek out advice from someone whose marriage appears to be running smoothly Make sure to ask yourself and your partner as many questions as possible regarding expectations for the marriage. And remember, there is no substitute for hard work.

Successful marriages last for a lifetime and bring endless joy and fulfillment, while marriages between incompatible people will most probably be short and will leave a painful trace in your memory. Not just that, but also bringing children into a marriage where the parents fight all the time creates a worse situation for the children and even more distress for the parents.

To make a marriage work over the long term is not that easy. We all have our faults, and no doubt we can all be hard to live with from time to time. Sure, it is possible to have a long and successful marriage.

Marriage is a complex puzzle, so take it seriously. Handle it with care. Nourish it with love and respect. Do not give up. Your focus and commitment will carry you through.

CHAPTER TWO

THE FUNDAMENTALS

Falling in love takes emotions, but staying in love is primarily the work of brain. Those individuals who marry at the prompting of their emotions and expect to go on autopilot mode cannot go very far in marriage. Love wears off quickly when the daily grind of life takes a toll on you.

To feel close to the person you married, you first have to trust them. That includes knowing that they are there for you when you need them. An intimate relationship is a supportive one. When you appreciate and encourage the person you love on a consistent basis, you are forming an intimate bond. Rejecting your spouse in any way is pulling away at those trust levels that marriage needs. Couples need and want to feel secure and emotionally involved with their partner.

It is quite ironic that couples feel closer and more loving towards each other the more they give of themselves in the marriage. Intimacy is not something that just happens—it is made. It takes two to become intimate, and it takes two to maintain intimacy in the marriage. If only one is working towards being close and the other is pulling away from getting close, then intimacy will not happen.

Intimacy is communicating on a deeper level than just talking about the weather. Many couples take this area of the relationship for granted and do not realize that their marriage actually thrives on intimacy.

Not growing together with the one you are married to is one of the underlying reasons for infidelity in marriage, not just physically, but emotionally as well. Emotional infidelity is becoming the new fad. It starts out innocently enough, but having an emotional involvement with someone other than your spouse is dangerous to the marriage. Couples do not need to go looking for someone who understands and appreciates them. All they really need to do is to be open and honest in their conversations with the person they married. So many couples don't want to work at their relationship, wrongly thinking that everything will work itself out. A marriage is like anything else in life—if you want it to last a significant amount of time, you must nourish and look after it.

What you put in is what you get out. And if you are not putting anything in, you cannot expect to get much out of it. Those couples who report a successful and extremely happy marriage also report actively taking an interest in each other and making an effort to ensure their marriage works.

Think back to when you first met your partner. Can you remember those giddy feelings of being crazily in love? We all know that this state of bliss cannot last forever, but you can still recapture those moments in your marriage today.

Part of staying in love is treating your partner as you would a friend. Just because someone is family doesn't give you the right to treat them badly. Even treating your partner as you would treat a stranger is probably better than how you treat each other now. We treat new people we meet with respect and courtesy. We would do well to treat the most important person in our lives in the same way.

Do you spend quality time together? Sometimes we can get so busy and caught up with daily living that we forget our partner. Take the time to rediscover each other and remember why you fell in love in the first place.

By doing all of the above things, you will have a stronger marriage and staying in love will be easily achieved.

With marriages failing at a rate that surpasses the 50 percent mark, you need to be sure that your decision is the right one. It's probably one of the most critical choices you will ever make.

So, how do you make that choice? How do you make a life determination so important that it will color every moment of the rest of your life?

Well, there are two schools of thought when it comes to making big life path choices. One is the concept of using logic to arrive at the choice—making a list of pros and cons, weighing the benefits and the risks, and then coming to a decision that makes the most practical sense.

The other way of thinking about choosing which path to go down at life's forks in the road is that you need to follow your heart. This philosophy says that our gut instincts will always lead us down the path that our subconscious knows is right for us.

When coming to as momentous conclusion as whether or not you are marrying the right person, you must engage the logical part of your brain along with your gut instinct.

To make your marriage a success, you must understand that it takes sacrifices; it takes patience; it takes tolerance and acceptance; it takes a mindset of trust and commitment. A marriage is the hardest commitment you can make. Why? Because you make a promise that you will spend the rest of your life together with this one person regardless of what will happen, until death does you apart. These days, many people seem to forget about their vows when problems start appearing in their relationships. They are so depressed about it that they take the shortcut and end the marriage altogether in a messy divorce. However, it really does not have to end that way.

Happiness and unhappiness are two sides of one coin. They are the emotions that we, as the owners, have power to choose which one we want to experience at a particular time. This may not seem obvious, as we are accustomed to the idea that our emotions happen to us. The truth is that we have the power to choose how we want to feel about something. The great news is that by having the correct mindset, nourishing your marriage will come naturally. It does not mean it is going to be effortless, but at least your mindset will steer you in the right direction.

To have the correct mindset towards your marriage, you need to keep in mind the following fundamental facts about marriages:

1.   A perfect marriage is a myth:

There is no such thing as "happily ever after" the fairy tale style. Yes, you can be happy ever after with your other half, but that requires a lot of work.

Be assured that there will be bumps and hurdles along the way. Every marriage has them.

People may pretend to sound as if they are in a fairy-tale-style relationship. If they actually believe that, it means they have not walked together far enough. Marriage goes through trying times early on. The grass appears to be greener on the other side.

When you are first starting out as a married couple, especially at a young age, many factors take a toll on you—e.g., adjusting to each other's habits and attitudes; bearing the love and burdens of child rearing; trying to make a nest for your family on a budget. Your relationship goes through trials as your children start to act up in their teenage years. Financial burdens and health challenges are big-ticket stress items. Most marriages break during this early phase of life.

If you manage to navigate through this phase, your marriage should become tepid. And the second phase begins. You start taking each other for granted. Boredom in the relationship sets in. You become very susceptive to outside interests. If you two don't take care of each other by growing together and taking an active interest in each other's lives, it's very easy to lose your spouse to infidelity or depression. Maintaining a strong intimate relationship is very crucial at this stage.

If you make it through the second phase, the rest of your life should be a no-brainer. You will look back at your trials and tribulations and find solace in knowing that you've got it made. And you'll also realize that it was not so bad. You'll rejoice in your family's triumphs.

At this point, it's not about individuals anymore. It is the collective achievements of the couple, their children, and grandchildren.

And this is the ultimate reward a successful marriage bears. If you break away from your marriage in the first two stages, you will never see the ultimate joy in being married.

2.   Nobody is perfect:

We hear that saying all the time, but often we don't realize it when it comes to our relationships. Your partner is not perfect, and neither are you. There is no point in seeking perfection in each other and putting your expectations up too high. Accept each other for who you are.

Stop expecting your spouse to become someone else. As we grow up in different environments, our belief systems and our habits to conduct daily activities of life are bound to be different. What is perfectly normal for one person may be very odd for the other person.

Once married, understand the "why and how" of your partner's behavior. By being critical and disrespectful, you will make a bad situation worse. Move from "what should be" to "what is." Your partner will respond to your expectations positively only if your requests come from genuine love.

Change because of fear in a marital relationship is not sustainable, and it does not create a healthy relationship. Bashing and ridiculing your partner will only spiral down your partner's confidence level.

Respect and work with what you got.

3.   Marriage is about compromises:

Having a happy marriage is more like a process rather than a destination. Keeping each other's needs in the forefront will bring you closer and help establish trust and respect. There is give and take, and there will be times when you have to give in to avoid a fight. You are two different individuals brought together, so there are bound to be lots of differences in likes and dislikes or in the way you view things. No matter how long you have "practiced" to keep your marriage flowing smoothly, you will still face new problems here and there. But hopefully by then you will have the correct mindset to overcome those problems easily.

4. Good communication is the key:

If there were only one piece of advice on how to save a marriage, good communication would be the answer. It is so critical that having an open, honest style of communication can often literally save broken relationships. Keep in mind that, with very few exceptions, both you and your partner are not mind readers. You need to tell each other how you feel about things so you both can deal with the problems accordingly.

5. Ego has no place in a marital relationship:

Get that hat off. You can impress rest of the world with the shield of ego. But inside your marital confines, ego has no place. If you choose to wear it, you will fail to be mindful, fair, and nonjudgmental. Your ego will get your relationship in trouble before you know it.

CHAPTER THREE

ARE YOU COMPATIBLE?

"How can I see if I'm compatible with someone?" is one of the most commonly asked questions among people before they propose marriage. Most people would agree it's a pretty important question, the answer to which will probably impact the rest of your life. How many people have gotten married who were incompatible with each other? Millions of people marry every year, and roughly half of those get divorced, many within the first five years. That sobering statistic says something.

The nation's high divorce rate may indicate many things, but one of those is almost certainly that too many couples get married when they are not compatible with one another. How many couples stay together even though they are not compatible? Again, there is no way of knowing for sure, but there are definitely some people who don't agree on very many things, yet go on to have strong, healthy marriages. Others, however, don't fare so well.

In any case, determining whether or not two people are compatible with each other before they get engaged would seem to be a desirable thing to do.

With that in mind, here are some great methods and tests that can help you discern if you and your partner are truly compatible with each other.

What is your level of education? Can your partner understand and appreciate your achievements? If not, soon you will find yourselves sitting in different camps looking for approval and appreciation of your capabilities elsewhere. If your partner is on the same page with you, then it's double the pleasure. I am not suggesting that you must have exactly the same level of education. However, you must have enough exposure and some interest in understanding each other's areas of interest. You must feel comfortable and good involving your spouse in your professional circles.

Do you like to spend much of your time the same way? For example, if one of you would rather enjoy a quiet afternoon listening to jazz and reading a novel, but the other would find their Saturday more enjoyable rock climbing El Capitan while blasting out AC/ DC on their iPod, that could point to incompatibility. How passionate you are about your activities and how likely you are to compromise in case you have to, is another key indicator of compatibility. For example, if you'd sooner chop off your toe with a broken beer bottle than give up your rock climbing, and your partner doesn't enjoy rock climbing, are you likely to make it together in the long haul? Think about that question for a while.

What are your respective attitudes toward money, and how is this reflected in your behavior? Are you a shopaholic? That may not go over too well if your partner is the frugal sort. Does one of you think about money with planned, long-term goals in mind, while the other can't see past their next paycheck? Money problems are at the root of many divorces today. By some estimates, they are the leading cause of divorce. It is important to reconcile any differences you may have about your personal monetary policies before you enter into a serious relationship that could lead to marriage.

What are your attitudes toward cleanliness, and is that reflected in the way you keep your respective houses, assuming you're not living together already? If one of you is a slob and the other neat and tidy, the organized one could be aggravated by the sloppy one. Such mismatched behavior patterns are not easy to change, and they can add tremendous stress to a relationship.

Here is a big one. Do you both want children? And if so, how many? If one partner really wants children and the other does not, your chances for a successful, long-term relationship are quite possibly doomed. This is something that is terribly difficult to overcome. If one partner does not want children, what are their reasons for their feelings? Is there a way to help them to overcome their objections?

These are some of the areas that you need to examine to determine if you can have a successful marriage. Just because a couple doesn't completely agree on one or more of these doesn't necessarily mean that they won't have a successful relationship, but it does mean the potential for friction in their relationship is that much higher.

The more areas you fundamentally disagree on, the longer and more difficult the road to a successful relationship will be. Conversely, near complete agreement in all of these areas does not guarantee compatibility and success in a marriage, but the odds are surely much greater.

CHAPTER FOUR

ARE YOU SURE?

Make sure that you are marrying for the right reasons. Life is different when you are in love with someone and not yet married to that person. You take special care to look good for each other. You always put your best foot forward. You are polite to each other. You are very attentive. You treat each other to sweet surprises— flowers, lavish dinners, show, and so forth.

Amazingly enough, people do not get to know each other before they enter into a marriage. People do not take the time to get to know one another before they begin a lifelong journey down a road that often leads to complex situations. Things change and people change when the security of the commitment is tied together by a marriage certificate. People relax into their old habits which were carefully put away during the dating at the beginning of the relationship.

There are several reasons why this continues to happen in our society. Once we make an emotional connection with that someone special, our critical abilities seem to take a very passive role. We are either dazzled by the brilliance we see in that person, or there are other benefits attached to the relationship that overrule any negative signals that come through our radar.

Too young and get involved sexually first. Many couples today are young people who become infatuated with each other thinking they have found true love. Tender puppy love sets in, and the next thing you know they have found the experience of a sexual encounter. And in most cases what spurs them to hold on to what they think is love is the disdain or disapproval of either of the parents. So they jump into a marriage when they are old enough because they want to prove their mom and dad wrong. Or they may do it as a reaction toward friends, for that matter, who have expressed a dislike for the partner their friend has chosen.

Getting older and time is running out. This reason has become more and more common in the current age group of thirty to forty-five. Generally, those who had found a relationship they thought was marriage-worthy would have gotten married by this time. Those from this age group who have not yet been married find that if they are going to have a child, they need to find a partner at lightning speed.

Loneliness is a great motivator for two people to jump into a relationship and/or marriage. With divorce rate percentages much higher than before, especially in middle-aged couples, people react to attention and latch onto a person because of the void they now have in their lives. After months or years in a relationship or marriage and the comfort of a partner, many people find themselves very lonely. At the first sign of attention or affection, they move quickly toward the comfortable feeling of another relationship so that the loneliness goes away.

Unfortunately, they find themselves lonely again because they married someone they did not really know and who they might not be compatible with.

CHAPTER FIVE

IS DIVORCE THE ONLY OPTION?

Nobody marries for reasons illustrated as required by professionals. People fall for looks, love, money, security, and so forth. All the different reasons to be married are well and good. But why do things look so different after tying the knot? Why do people feel as if they are suffocating after the marriage when they felt quite comfortable in the relationship for the longest time? Why do infidelities ruin near-perfect marriages? Why in the face of illness, death, or financial challenges do people take the easy way out—divorce?

Divorce does not, and cannot make anybody happy; it is a temporary solution to get away from a very stressful situation.

The sole reason for this sudden change lies in perception. People don't necessarily change, but their roles change; the expectations that were not thought through, before suddenly become overwhelmingly stressful. Lack of commitment and lack of focus can confuse couples. They find that the only easy way out is to get out of relationship through divorce.

Let us take a look at some ordinary human beings whose lives come tumbling down at the first sight of challenge in married life. The following stories are real. You as a third party might see the scenario differently than the actual players of these stories. Get your antennas up and activate your critical abilities so that you can benefit from the mistakes of these victims of innocent human behavior.

❖

Real Life Story # 1

A Case of Non-Communicated Expectations:

Karen had offered temporary shelter to a friend's friend, named Leonard, who was moving from LA to Arlington, Virginia. Leonard was moving because of his job transfer. Karen and Leonard were both very good-looking young individuals. Instantly, they fell in love. They were both professionals and both available—meaning no other strings attached.

They were excellent mates in bed. They had never experienced such satisfying sex before. They surprised everyone with the announcement, "We are married." On a four-day cruise to the Caribbean within two months of the beginning of their courtship—or after a two-month sex marathon— they got married on the boat.

Soon after marriage, they began to find out that they had diametrically opposing personalities. They started bickering over every little thing, and the conflicts got deeper and deeper. Leonard had no desire to do anything else but go to work, flip TV channels, and lie on the couch. He was a lazy man and a total slob. Karen, on the other hand, was the kind of person who is very clean, organized, and full of zest for life.

In blind attraction to Leonard, Karen had distanced herself from her friends. Now when she realized what a mess she had on her hands, in distress, she started spending time with her friends again. It was then that she realized there was nothing in common between the two of them. She did not know anything about this man's background and his interests in life. All she knew was that he was an excellent sex mate, incredibly good looking, and willing to marry her.

Leonard really had no complaints about Karen except that she was constantly criticizing him and putting him down. After four months of marriage, Karen asked Leonard to move out. He did. Their affair did not last to see its first anniversary. They were divorced.

When a marriage is established on a weak foundation and there is no measure of compatibility at work, it cannot be a wholesome marriage. If sex is the reason for marriage—or the reason for divorce—obviously, there is nothing else to look for to support the marriage.

How much time do you spend in bed when married? I am by no means undermining the importance of sex in life. You have to work, carry out daily activities to support your life, and have a social presence too. So all these other activities weigh heavily as well, and then you start to find out who the real person your partner is. Sex is certainly important in married life, but marriage is much more than that. You can seek help to enhance your sexual life if it becomes an issue. That is just one area. If you have totally opposite personalities, you will find yourself angry, bickering, fighting, and miserable.

If you go through the dating period with all your expectations of each other fully laid out and properly communicated, you will probably give each other a chance to settle down in marriage. If the expectations are not clear to your partner, how can he/she be expected to satisfy you?

Suddenly, Karen expected a wholesome marriage. When she did not see what she probably had in the back of her mind, baffled and stressed, she called it quits.

Could this marriage work?

Sure, had Karen and Leonard spent some time envisioning and communicating their life together before taking the plunge, it would have given them a chance to accept each other for who they really are. And once they did get married, why rush for a divorce? They were both educated and career-oriented.

No two individuals are alike. They should have looked at each other's abilities as an asset to their marriage. They should have given a chance to their marriage. They should have communicated the reasons of their frustrations with each other. People do step up to plate. Karen focused on all of Leonard's negative traits. She did not give their marriage a chance to survive. This marriage did not have even a chance because Karen and Leonard did not bother to understand each other. It takes two to have the mindset, vision and the desire to make it work.

Real Life Story# 2

The Not So Compatible Couple:

Roger is a real-life character. He is a reasonably well-off guy. He owns a limousine business in downtown DC. He is a well-dressed, good-looking, and mild-mannered man in his fifties. He does not have a formal, college-level education. He might not even have a high school diploma. His first wife died of cancer five years ago. She worked for the federal government for more than twenty years. He adored her. He has a son and three grandchildren from that marriage. Roger loves his grandchildren very dearly. He got attached to them even more after he lost his wife.

How do I know all this? Roger bought and sold many real estate properties through me over the time of about twelve years. He met a woman who was working for the IRS, holding a pretty responsible job. Her name was Irene. I had the opportunity to meet Irene. She was finishing up the tail end of her thesis. Soon enough, Irene is supposed to become Dr. Irene.

Irene and Roger took trips together. After a courtship of three months, they got engaged and the wedding date was all set in about three months. Shelly, Roger's niece and goddaughter, called me up one day. Shelly is also my real estate client. She asked me, "What do you think of Irene?" I replied that I had not known her long enough to form an opinion. The woman was well-read. She was never married. Roger's niece Shelly was quite perturbed by the developing relationship between Roger and Irene. She told me that she was very concerned and she did not approve of her uncle marrying Irene.

Roger was very lonely, so he married Irene. Two months after the wedding, they had separated and were looking to finalize the divorce quickly. Roger asked to meet with me to sell off a couple of his properties.

Roger shared with me that this relationship was all stress for him. He felt that he had been manipulated by Irene. She was extremely demanding and always put him down for being uneducated. She did not like his side of the family. He was not allowed to visit his grandchildren. He was not allowed to talk about his first wife whom he lost to cancer. He was never Mr. Right when they visited Irene's sisters and her mother.

She always found faults with whatever he did or did not do. She always put him down. She had told some fibs about Roger's business to her family that Roger did not verify for Irene. She had bragged that Roger had a fleet of twenty limousines while he had only five and he chauffeured one himself.

Let's examine this marriage:

Roger alleviated his loneliness by marrying Irene. But he lost everything else he loved—including visiting his grandchildren, which was his greatest joy after losing his first wife. As Irene found faults with his very being, he started to feel miserable. He could not put on a show of being the businessman that Irene wanted him to be. They never had any conversations that explored what they expected out of their relationship. They never visualized the changes Roger would have to make to accommodate his new wife. Irene never asked any direct questions about Roger's business. She just assumed that he was a big businessman, when in reality he was a simple, hard-working man. So she had to put on a charade about Roger's business to match her ego. They both were uncomfortable with each other's real self.

Could this marriage work?

It is quite possible that they could make it together. Instead of running to divorce, they should have given their union a chance. Once they were married, they should have exhausted their other options.

Both of them should have put their true cards on the table and faced the reality of each other. Once they open up to "what is," the stress caused by assumptions and false expectations could dissipate. Irene's ego could also be adjusted knowing the true gentleman that Roger was. They were both self-sufficient. They needed each other's kind company and not a whole lot more. So sure, they could have grown old together, loving and supporting each other.

Real Life Story #3

A Collision of Belief Systems:

Salim and Liz went to college together. They were good friends. Salim came from a very religious Muslim family. Liz was Jewish and her parents' only child. She decided to take a job in Washington DC, and Salim was already settled in the area with his family. Liz and Salim kept seeing each other and found themselves in love. In spite of opposition from Liz's family, they decided to get married. The marriage took place with all the traditions and ceremonies of the Muslim faith. Liz's family did not participate.

They purchased a beautiful condominium in McLean, Virginia, and seemed like a very contented and happy couple. They had their first daughter during their first year of marriage. Liz needed help to raise their little girl, Karen, so they moved back into Salim's family home. Salim's mother and little sisters helped take care of Karen, while Liz went back to work.

Liz did not fit in with the family. It was a very close-knit family with a lot of extended family members constantly visiting. Liz was expected to behave like a typical Muslim wife with a head covering on in the presence of senior male members. She started to feel suffocated in this very staunchly religious Muslim environment.

Salim had showed no signs of being a religious type of guy when they were dating. However, after the birth of their daughter, Salim suddenly felt the urge to raise his daughter in a strict Muslim family environment.

Liz expressed her desire to live independently away from the family. Even though they moved out to their own condominium, Salim could not put his parents and his siblings out of the equation. He wanted his family to stay very much involved with the upbringing of their daughter. Liz and Salim could not compromise on this issue. They mutually agreed to part ways and filed for divorce.

Could this marriage work?

This one had a tough chance. Liz and Salim came from very distinctly different belief systems. People coming from different cultures and different faiths have a lot of difficulty accepting their new environment. Since Salim was raised with traditions and strong cultural values, he should not have married Liz.

His religion, his family, and his culture was part of who he was. He should have taken stock of his own value and belief system; he should have communicated his expectations to Liz before proposing.

The only way Liz could have survived in that marriage was if she had a "doormat" type personality. She didn't. Once the initial sizzle of the marriage quieted down, realities surfaced.

Real Life Story # 4

A Case of Marrying Too Young:

Rebecca and William, now twenty-one, have three children. Rebecca got pregnant while in high school. She had her first baby at age seventeen.

With the birth of their second child at age nineteen, they got married. William had to work two jobs to take care of his family. They rented a basement from Mr. Stanley—a family friend. Rebecca stayed home.

Mr. Stanley was a divorced man. His three children were grown. They had left home. Mr. Stanley was an electrician. He worked as a contractor for a big company. He had a flexible work schedule.

Frustrated and not having enough money to go around, Rebecca frequently beat up her crying children. Neighbors noticed a nuisance in that household.

Mr. Stanley started to visit with Rebecca, first with innocent intentions of helping her out with the children, and then it developed into a convenient affair. He helped Rebecca financially from time to time.

One day, William came home sick. He did not go to his second job. To his amazement, he found his wife in bed with Mr. Stanley. In a rage, William beat up Mr. Stanley. Rebecca begged for William's forgiveness that evening. But the affair had been going on for a while.

William one day packed up and left his family.

Marrying too young is a mistake.

Marriages that take place in the ages of twenty five to thirty two are more stable and long-lasting than teen marriages. Teens are not ready to handle the challenges of marriage. Raising children and earning a living can be very stressful for young individuals. Every little problem can blow up into fights. Fighting stress can lure a person down the wrong path.

Teen relationships are common in today's world. Adolescence is the most important stage for youngsters to make their future colorful and to become responsible citizens in society.

To help a teen who wants to get married, you can help them explore a different scenario (role playing) before it happens as a way of preparing them. One such example would be about meeting the responsibilities of being a parent, providing for the family, and spending time with the family.

To help a young teen who chooses to get married, you can help them outline their short and long-term goals and offer to act as a mentor to give them guidance to deal with the different problems that will come up. Most teen marriages may not last because their minds are still growing and they don't have enough experience in life and the choices out there for them to make a decision to be married.

Only a strong household with nurturing parents can provide the security that young teens need so that they don't seek false security by marrying someone when they are still children themselves.

Real Life Story #5

A Case of Confusion, Immaturity, and Lack of Communication/ Commitment:

Judy and Ken got introduced on the Internet. They met each other several times and found each other compatible in all respects. Ken was twenty-nine, a young orthopedic surgeon who joined a group of professionals with a very lucrative financial package. Ken was in Chicago and Judy in California. Judy was an only child and came from a very protective and wealthy family of professionals. Ken was the only son in his family. Both of his parents were school teachers. Ken had two sisters who wished to follow in their brother's footsteps. Ken's parents had to make a lot of personal sacrifices to get him through medical school. They were a very close-knit family.

Two months prior to the wedding, Ken's dad had a heart attack and did not survive. Ken's family was distraught. However, the wedding took place anyway. Judy moved to Chicago. They both moved into a beautiful new home.

Ken's mom and two sisters were constantly in touch with Ken. Ken had stepped into the fatherly role with his sisters, lecturing and advising them to study harder and take care of their mom.

Judy felt that Ken's family was in the way of their relationship. They were either talking to him on the phone or Ken was constantly worrying about them. Judy started to assume that Ken no longer cared for her. Ken was wrapped up in work and his grieving family. He really loved Judy very much. However, Judy did not see it.

She felt like an outsider. She gave him subtle signals that she was feeling lonely and ignored. For instance, she would leave for a long walk when it was time for Ken to come home. Ken wasn't happy with Judy's newfound love of walks. Not much was exchanged between them; they avoided each other. One thing leading to another, they filed for divorce within five months of their wedding.

Could this marriage be saved?

Most definitely, yes! Judy and Ken needed to communicate. Judy needed to understand that Ken was going through a very rough patch. Time is a great healer—she should have known that. Maybe they should have delayed getting married. Ken should have sorted things out with his family first. Once they were together, they should have paid attention to each other. Judy was not working. She had too much time on her hands to think about things. It was a very critical time to establish their married relationship. They needed to believe in each other. Judy needed to be more understanding. Instead of Judy feeling like an outsider, she could have offered to try to help ease Ken's pain. Ken's mistake was that he ignored what Judy was trying to say. Instead of getting a handle on things, they chose to avoid each other. They drifted apart.

When one person feels down, the other one should take on the responsibility to lift the other up. Unless you stop worrying about who's right and who's wrong, you just aren't going to solve a single thing. Let me be frank—when a relationship is suffering, who cares who's at fault, fix it!

Real Life Story #6

A Case of Race and Color Issues:

In the summer of 1983, I met Jeff and Susan Spencer. They had a nice colonial single-family home with extensive landscaping and a nice, big in-ground pool. I lived in a townhouse community with my husband and two children, one street up from the Spencers. Jeff was mostly gone on travel. I saw Susan with two little girls who were roughly the same age as our two sons.

Jeff and Susan had adopted the girls from southern India as they could not have children of their own. Susan and I usually ran into each other at our neighborhood grocery store and at the common tot-lots of our little com- munity. From a common acquaintance, we became good friends rather quickly. Susan and I took strolls together along with our little kiddies. The kids seemed to get along just great. Susan and I would share Indian and American recipes and learn about each other's culture.

We had a good run of about two months like that. One day Susan called me up. She had just come back from the grocery store and was very upset. She said, "Sukh, I've just had it with these people. Don't you think my two girls are beautiful? In the grocery store, a white couple called me a whore today. Erica and Sharon were with me picking strawberries and this couple passed by and whispered 'whore.' I heard it loud and clear. I confronted them and they gave me dirty looks and walked away." Susan was outraged, to say the least. "And this is not the first time it happened. I do get strange looks from time to time, but this…" Susan continued to tell me.

"The other day, a middle-aged black man made a dirty pass at me. Am I supposed to walk around with a note on my forehead that I have adopted these children from India?"

I was truly speechless. My mind was racing through Susan's heartache and her husband's possible reaction to it…and the poor little girls. Next time we met, Susan poured her heart out. She told me that her husband had already been feeling guilty about this adoption. He had been refusing to go out in public with the children. Susan said that it was their joint decision to adopt. Her husband had medical problem and could not have children.

They tried to have children for many years. Jeff had hinted to Susan that if she wanted a divorce, he would understand. Susan suggested they could adopt. Jeff's mother was fine with the idea of adoption until they adopted the girls from India.

Susan's mother-in-law had refused to accept the children as her grandchildren. And Jeff was not willing to say anything to his mother. Susan did not get along with her mother-in-law. Was this the only issue, or was there something else at play? I never found out. Within a year of this episode, Susan and Jeff had sold the house and divorced. Erica and Sharon stayed with Susan.

What went wrong?

This divorce was clearly a product of many complex issues. Jeff did not seem to be involved in the adoption process. Susan either adopted without consulting Jeff about the details, or Jeff might have given his okay to go ahead with the process. Jeff's mother's refusal to see the children or accept them because they were not Caucasian had a significant role in the breakdown of their marriage. Clearly not all major players were on the same page.

Susan's husband was on business trips all the time. It seems that what happened with his family was a distant thing that did not impact him. He was not keen on strengthening the relationship between his mother and his wife. The role of all players in a household should be very clear and acceptable to all parties involved. Being a couple is more than a full-time job. This marriage was hanging by a frail thread.

This is so typical of marriage relationships. Once couples slide into their comfortable positions, they get so relaxed that they forget to keep a tab on their marital relationship.

Couples cannot afford to be complacent about a rift springing up between a husband and a wife. It has to be handled right away.

Real Life Story #7

A Case of Lies and Mistrust:

Harriet and John were high school sweethearts. They parted for college. John went to pursue a degree in veterinary science. Harriet graduated from a local college in sociology. After graduating, they got married.

Two years later John was in a bad car accident and was carried to the hospital. Harriet found out that John was HIV positive. When asked, John told Harriet the truth that he had known it all along. He now shared that he had experienced a different kind of lifestyle while in college and had contracted HIV. He didn't tell Harriet earlier because he thought that if he told her, she would not marry him. Harriet filed for a divorce as soon as John came back from the hospital.

Hmmmmm!

Harriet did not divorce John just because he was HIV positive. How could John keep such a big secret of having an alternative lifestyle and carry on with her at the same time all those years? For Harriet, this constituted a grand betrayal of many innocent years of friendship with John. Harriet's soul was bruised, her trust shattered.

Harriet had assumed that John was still the same young man who happened to be the love of her sweet teenage years. Obviously, John loved her enough to come back to Harriet to marry her. John and Harriet come from different value systems. They are fundamentally different. They probably had not chalked out a shared vision of their life together as a married couple. They did not verbalize their expectations of each other, so there was no clear understanding of each other's value system.

Too many people rush into marriage without realizing what they are getting into.

**When you know that you have made a mistake in your
dealings with your significant other, you must admit that
to your partner and put all your cards on the table.**

**Level with yourself about your feelings. Level with
each other. Ask for acceptance and forgiveness.**

**If it is not achieved at this point, it never will be.
Obviously, if your value system is not the same, you are
going to have to work very hard at your relationship.**

Most people get married for selfish reasons only. No one says,
"If I marry you, I'll be the most miserable person on earth—let's get
married." No, you got married because you believed that the marriage
would make you happy. If you did not believe that, you would not get
married.

Yet, after the wedding you discover that things aren't all honey and
roses. You find out that you aren't always happy, and you aren't always
satisfied. In fact, the closer you get to someone the more potential they
have to hurt you and you them. You argue more with people you love
than anyone else.

Maturity in marriage is where you realize that you have committed
yourself to someone else in a way that is reminiscent of patriotism. It's
a feeling that anchors you with your principles. When you can pledge
yourself to another person, your marriage has finally matured. This isn't
easy, and it is not something that is actually done when you got married.
It's an act of maturity that comes with your value system.

When you get married you make certain vows. But a vow isn't
meaningful until you are forced to keep it. When things get tough,
that's when the vow begins to have meaning for you. How many people
make all sorts of promises only to break them in divorce and other ways?
Too many! Those marriages never had true commitment.

When your love and your promises are put to the test that is where
the depth of your relationship reveals itself. Your relationship is mature
when you can look each other in the eye as your marriage stands on

rocky and uncertain ground and then say, "I made some promises when we got married, and I intend to keep them. I'm committed to you, and I'm committed to making this relationship work."

At some point your marriage must be transformed from the selfishness that originally existed to the commitment that will keep you together. Feeling committed to someone when everything is going well is not a true demonstration of commitment. When things seem to be falling apart, when you feel insecure, disappointed, and unloved perhaps, and yet you can still remain committed, that is a good demonstration of commitment.

I've never seen a marriage that didn't go through turbulent times. It is these times, and remaining committed through them, that gives a relationship the specialness and strength that you first sought when you got married to begin with.

What you want in a relationship doesn't come until the relationship has weathered some fairly serious storms. It is the difficult times that make a relationship great. So if you can remain committed during these trying and desperate times, you'll get the relationship you first sought when you chose to get married.

<hr>

CHAPTER SIX

WHY DO MARRIAGES FAIL?

The stories I have cited in the foregoing pages demonstrate human frailty. The characters are our everyday men and women who start out married life with all good intentions. At the first sight of a problem, we are baffled. We question our own decisions.

People who divorce quickly are the people who are short-sighted. Every time they start out again, they face similar problems. And they run again. They make their baggage heavier. They think they can find happiness elsewhere. They fail to understand that happiness comes with your own attitudes toward life.

Every marriage goes through a maze; it is different and specific for every couple. If the players don't understand the challenges and lack the resolve to deal with situations as they come, then they conveniently quit. To simplify this great puzzle of life, let us discuss the root causes of failure of a marriage. I find the following three reasons responsible:

1. Choosing a wrong mate
2. Immaturity in handling everyday issues
3. Abuse—emotional, physical, or substance use

Choosing a Wrong Mate:

Marry whosoever you want to; marry for whatever reasons you want to; but understand that if you are not compatible with your mate, expect an uphill battle.

People frequently make the mistake of not doing their homework before getting married. If you plan a journey, you plan ahead. You keep in mind the purpose and destination of the journey. You arrange the neces- sities required for travel. You arrange money to meet your needs. You preplan for excursions. You carefully select people you take the journey with to make it more enjoyable.

When embarking upon a journey of life time, do you comprehend the complexity of married life?

If you do not start this journey with the right partner who shares your aspirations and dreams, you will be lost in no time. You will only be rolling along without a definitive direction. When you stumble upon a challenge, which happens frequently in married life, your marriage will spin out of control.

How long can a marriage last like that—in confusion, misery, and boredom? That's why affairs start. That's why fights starts—blaming each other. Finances become messed up. If you have children in marriage, they watch all that. When they grow up, they will end up on the same path. Why? Because that's all they witnessed; that's all they know.

Marriages founded on lies cannot be stable. Some people have the wrong notion that if your partner marries you, all problems will be over. Have you come across women pretending to be pregnant? What is the motivation there? They just want to trap their partner. People lie about their assets and liabilities only as a trap. But the consequences are serious. When the victim partner finds out the reality of the matter, not only is he or she angry beyond measure, but your partner will also lose trust in you. Forget about getting any respect from your partner. You must put all your cards on the table. Level with your partner about your thoughts. Level with your partner before going into a marital commitment. Your religious, cultural, and ethnic beliefs can collide. Love happens. It does not take much to fall in love. Logic sets in a little later than romance. For people who grow up in an environment of strong faith and traditions, that lifestyle becomes an intrinsic part of them. If you are that individual and if you fall in love with a person who does not believe in your faith or your value system, you will have an uphill battle throughout your life. Love for your newfound partner may be strong enough to overlook this major issue in the beginning, but as soon as you settle into life, your partner will feel alienated and suffocated in that rigid environment.

Couples who do not explore their belief systems before getting married can get trapped into marriage that they later regret. The story of Liz and Salim is a perfect example.

Immaturity in Handling Everyday Issues:

Statistics suggest that 70 percent of divorces come within the first seven years of marriages. This staggering number indicates that half of marriages fail because spouses can't live with each other anymore. It indicates that a couple is burned out. They fail to see each other's perspective. They see divorce as a quick fix to their misery. They think that they don't love each other anymore. This is an absurd notion.

The fact is that you are in the process of developing a new family unit. Both of you will have to adjust to each other's specific expectations. You will have to form a new platform where your own nuclear identity will conceive and evolve as a family unit. And by no means is it going to be easy. These are challenging times. Your focus and commitment will lead the way for this formation. The trick is that you have to learn to adjust your expectations. You have to accept your spouse for who he/she is. You have to communicate emphatically.

Since we all come from different environments, we are bound to be different. We are bound to have disagreements. We are bound to be defensive of our behavior. It's all right. What really causes problems in marriage is when we get stuck in our points of view. We try to prove ourselves to be right, which simply means your partner has to be wrong.

Who wants to be wrong? This leads to finger pointing and arguments. It accomplishes nothing. We bicker about whose fault it is. We should worry about finding a solution. To be honest with you, most of us are idiots in this area. We're more interested in defending a position than we are in solving it.

Most marriages are ruined because people have flawed perception regarding marriage. People fight over "yours and mine" when everything should be "ours." There is no fifty-fifty rule in marriage. It's all about 100+ percent. If both partners give 100+ percent of themselves, their time, their abilities, and their assets/liabilities to marriage, there will never be a problem.

When you get married, the very act of doing so meant that you gave up any right to "your rights." Marriage is a unity of two people and all that they are. As long as you hold selfishly to "your rights," you can't achieve the true objective of a marriage—the unity of a man and woman.

It's very selfish, naïve, and fatal to marriage to think, "If this doesn't work out, we can just get a divorce." A marriage needs a burning desire to work through any problem, overcome any obstacle, and defeat any trial. If you're hoping that your marriage will be eternal bliss, you are sadly mistaken.

All marriages have struggles; and it is the struggles that bind us closer together; propel us to think outside the box; force us to reevaluate our priorities, and help us focus on the true riches in life.

"I've got to have a life that is separate from my marriage." This is a very, very dangerous attitude to have in a marriage. Typically, it is men who feel they need to have this more than women do. But either way, having a life outside of your marriage is disastrous for the marriage. Does that mean that you can't do anything without your spouse? No. Just don't exile your mate from a part of your life. That breeds mistrust and suspicion. Another danger is forming a mental island that only you go to. This is often the result of problems within the marriage, and you mentally escape by going to that place in your mind and life that your mate can't come to. It can lead you to depression. It could be a fantasy world where you mentally fantasize about other men or women, or dream of a world where your mate is not. This leads to a dangerous way of thinking, and it will eventually spill over into reality. Creating this mental island is the first step to having an affair or moving toward divorce. When your spouse has a problem, then so do you.

Letting go of intimacy, causes problems. It happens when one partner is busy raising the children or busy making a living that couples slide into a period where they overlook the importance of "our time"—time spent together. They develop a routine that is mutually acceptable for a very short time. But if they don't break the cycle and pay attention to each other, they are risking the health of their relationship.

Intimacy is not just sexual in nature; it lies in acknowledging each other, appreciating each other, physical bonding, and staying interested in each other's routine work.

Sexual drive changes at a varying degree with different adults. When you start looking out for what you need and ignore the needs of your partner, it will create an emotional rift. You will drift apart. You always have to keep tabs on what your partner's needs are. Otherwise, couples will become involved in activities that take them away from their partner just to stay busy. Unintended, but surely soon enough they will no longer need each other, and meaningless activities will take the place of the intimacy that they needed.

Notice that couples out of child-rearing age often slip into these lapses. When that becomes routine, couples erroneously think that they are not in love with each other anymore. One thing leads to another, and they drift into different camps and spark relationships with new acquaintances. It is a dangerous game.

A personal friend of mine, let's call her Peggy, had an ailing and aging mother who lived down south in Florida. Peggy is in her late fifties. She is not the only child. She has three siblings who live closer to her mother. Her father passed away a while ago.

Three years in a row, Peggy stayed with her mother for several months at a time. Her husband Joe did not like her staying away from home for such lengths of time. During her lengthy absence during the third year, Joe filed for divorce on the basis of "abandonment." They were married for fifteen years.

We all will have situations in life where we will have such strong challenges that we will ignore the importance of physical and emotional union in marriage; left ignored for a while, this will cause your relationship to decline and ultimately fail. Divorces during middle age and later in life are the result of unintended behavior.

Abuse—Emotional, Physical, or Substance:

Regardless of whether the drug in question is alcohol or something else, addiction can easily ruin a marriage. Aside from increasing the risk of violent behavior, there is no question that someone who is addicted to drugs will have a hard time with emotional and spiritual bonding. Even if you are not the one addicted, you would need professional help to cope with your wounded marriage.

What about the one who is addicted? Try explaining the damage they are doing. Only the family of that unfortunate one can understand the pain, the stress, the strife, and all the misery that comes with drug use. Normal life is over for that family. The marriage is over even without a divorce. The drug user lives in a different and a superficial reality.

I came across a great loan officer who later became victim to drug use. He was a very respectable, hardworking young man in his late twenties. He was earning a fantastic living. He commanded full knowledge of his profession and offered brilliant solutions to his clients. I believed in him like many other realtors did.

I don't know when or why, but at some point he started to use drugs. I witnessed a very painful transformation in that young man's life. When my clients chose him to be their banker, I was assured of money in the bank. But now he was holding files for processing mortgage loans, did not process them at all, and kept telling lies to his clients that the loans were doing fine and he had no problem closing the loans on scheduled dates.

To his clients' total dismay, many of those loans were not even put into processing. He did not even open the files. It just took about three months to see the exact picture. He was using drugs. He was making rubbish statements to put out fires. As his superiors found out the reality of his state of mind, he was instantly fired from the job.

He is ruined for life. The last thing I heard is that he is living on the streets of Manhattan—a homeless man. His wife, who still lives in the area, has nothing to do with him. This man has deteriorated from a successful mort- gage loan officer to a homeless man. This is what drug use can do to a person.

If your spouse is addicted to a chemical substance, you are probably missing all kinds of things in the marriage. This may include emotional support, financial support, as well as any connection at a deeper level that you would have with a healthy mate. While support groups cannot take the place of a spouse, they can still give you a chance to talk to others going through similar situations. This will give you some time to sort out your own feelings, as well as consider what you can do to help your spouse get free of the addiction.

When you ask, "How do you save your marriage from drug abuse?" most people will recommend drug counseling. If you are not the one addicted, you will still need an enormous amount of emotional and spiritual support. Once the drugs are out of the picture, you may be able to finally enjoy all of the wonderful things that come with a healthy marriage.

So far as physical and mental abuse is concerned, I really have no defense mechanism to offer. Such abuse gives superpowers to the aggressor and reduces the victim to nothing. The only way such a marriage can come to terms is if the abused partner somehow gets up on their feet, looks in the eye of the abuser, and tells him/her "No more," and then takes charge of life by doing things differently.

There is no balance in a marriage where abuse rules. One is better off getting away from the aggressor as quickly as possible. Children are better off away from such an environment. Witnessing or participating in such a horrific environment is not healthy. Unless the abuser comes to his or her senses either through punishment by law or counseling or just wakes up one morning realizing that what has been going on is hideously wrong, I encourage the victim to seek separation and protect yourself and your family.

———————◆———————

PART TWO

FINDING A COMPATIBLE MATE—THE PROCESS

We must find the roots of our behavior if we seek change. We can surely steer the direction of our destiny if we know the path that leads to the present. This takes the right mindset and conviction. When our subconscious mind and conscious-self come to terms with each other, it allows us to execute plans and take action. This will in turn propel our belief system and create confidence and guidance.

CHAPTER SEVEN

KNOW YOURSELF

Marriages that last through the early years stand a good chance of success; only if couples give themselves a chance to succeed. Nonetheless, wrong unions create turmoil in the lives of everyone involved. With divorce, everyone leaves with heavier baggage. There are no winners, only losers. It affects the human psyche in many ways. It shatters one's confidence; it bruises one's soul. Divorce just changes a person. Therefore, divorce should be used as a last resort, not a quick fix to your problems.

Most people jump to marriage because they "fell in love." Feeling of being in love is not enough to sustain a life long journey. Feeling of love withers away when life starts to throw challenges your way. Nobody is immune to life's challenges. Some have more of it than others.

When things do not go right— when our expectations are not met; we start blaming each other.

Thus the seed of mistrust germinate, and becomes the root of troubles in our relationships.

Before taking a plunge of taking a relationship into marriage, you must understand that there are three essential elements to a good solid marriage:

Selecting the right person to marry is very crucial to a long happy journey of life. So find out who you are at present, and where you are headed in life. Therefore, know your aspirations, and know your expectations.

Second most important element entails sticking it out during the highs and lows of life. Do not go from relationship to relationship. In every relationship, you will find stuff that you would again want to run from. Why not keep the one you chose the first time around and stick to it. Handle and guard your relationship with the utmost care.

Thirdly, understand that love is very elusive in nature. When you first fall in love, it is love beyond measure. But then life happens and you may hate the same person beyond measure. When you and your spouse are willing to make it work, it will. When you put all your cards on the table and level with each other about your feelings, your decision to honor your commitment to each other will open the fountain of love again. Keep working on it. You will find contentment by doing the right thing, and that is happiness.

Know Your Package:

This chapter is fundamentally very important in the process of establishing parameters for finding a good, compatible partner. It is important to first know about yourself and your package.

What is in your package?

It is everything that you are today—your personality traits with all your strengths and weaknesses. You are the unique *you*. You are the "end product" of something you inherited and had no control over, and that was your environment. Your family, school, religion, the socioeconomic makeup of your community at large, and your genealogy gets the credit for making you the "unique you." That is your package.

Why is it so important?

Your prospective partner has a package too. If your partner in marriage has a package that becomes a burden on you, you will burn out really fast. You will quickly lose your enthusiasm for the relationship. Often, people discover themselves later on that their paths don't go side by side, and in fact, their paths may go in opposite directions.

Most of the time, troubles in marriage stem from the lack of knowledge of what you want in life. We do not think long and hard about our own package. Some habits that we form growing up may or may not be desirable as adults. You may need to take a critical look at whether or not your habits need tweaking.

Many marriages dissolve because they have trouble maintaining the lives they had imagined they would have with each other. If two partners are pulling in different directions, life quickly becomes unbearable.

So what is a good marriage?

A good marriage should always be stimulating for both persons involved and should cause each other to look forward to another day with your partner.

It should provide a union that doesn't erase one's individuality.

In order to find the right compatible person to marry, one must ask, "Who am I?" Then you can move on to the next step of finding someone compatible.

◆━━━◆━━━◆

CHAPTER EIGHT

SELF-ANALYSIS

Unarguably, the toughest of all analysis is the self-analysis. The sole purpose of this chapter is to raise your awareness of the self. You will ask some serious questions of yourself in the privacy of your own world—the world that shaped you; the world that involved all those people who played a significant role in your life. Understand that you are the "end product" of that world.

The foregoing chapters shed some light on common marital problems. Most of the problems can be avoided if we keep our expectations real. We cannot change others, but we definitely have control over what we do. It's just like being a safe driver on the road. We constantly learn new behaviors every day. With our fast-paced social environment, we modify ourselves to meet the challenges, knowingly or unknow-

ingly. Thus we evolve over time.

If we have awareness of who we are or what we *are*, we will make conscious choices to be who or what we want *to be*. Therefore, obtaining self-knowledge is a fundamental step to finding out who you are—and who you are not. This analysis will reveal your entire package. If we understand the roots of issues in our lives, we can definitely take better charge of life.

Self examination will benefit you in three ways: 1. You will identify your strengths. 2. You will acknowledge your weaknesses. 3. You will use this knowledge to create your vision of your own future.

Creating a vision for your life will put you on a positive path. It will create a mindset of thinking that whatever you want in life is within your grasp. Once you develop a positive attitude and focus on your intentions, you will find and develop ways to achieve it.

The future belongs to those who think about it; who prepare for it; for others, it just happens.

———◆———

Identify Your Strengths and Weaknesses:

Connecting with your strengths is about learning how to acknowledge your own gifts, accept compliments graciously, and to present yourself confidently as the extraordinarily unique artist that you are. Identifying your weaknesses is about preparing yourself to amend the parts you don't like.

It is impossible to change everything that is not so desirable about you. We have to come to terms with what cannot be changed, and we should reshape, mold, or relearn, when and whatever we can. This is an epic task, but if you can accomplish it now before entering into the next phase of your life—the married life—then you will have earned a license to a happy and prosperous future.

In order to evaluate yourself, you will need to become a third eye—a separate entity. Look at yourself from outside to inside and inside to outside. Check your baggage. See what you have in it.

1.   Examine Your Physical Self:

Examine what is your impression of your physical appearance. Are you tall, medium, or short in height? Are you pleasantly plump, fat, or skinny bones? Do you have a physical disability visible or not so visible to the outer world? How is your skin tone? You don't have to be critical about your physical self to a point that it brings you down or makes your head swell. Just be aware of it.

I am sure that you have a good idea how others perceive you. Parents look at their children through a very different mirror than rest of the world does. You can't always go by the hype you got growing up with your parents and grandparents.

Your schoolmates may have a different perception of you—a result of envy, immaturity, and a general teenage silly behavior. As a grown person, you are none of that. You might have developed some sort of complex— superiority or inferiority as a result of your childhood encounters. It could actually impact you in a very positive or a very negative way. Shake it all off. As a mature adult, before you get married, you must know the social rating of your physical appearance.

But, why? — it is a fair question. If you choose a partner who is diametrically superior or inferior looking when compared with you, you will have social challenges to face most of your life. People—friends, relatives, and coworkers will constantly remind you that "you did not deserve…" or that "you deserved better." People will talk in front of you, behind your back, or in whispers. No matter how strongly you feel about your partner, hearsay will catch up with you. It will bug you. It will impact you. Your attitude will reflect your anguish. It will have an impact on your relationship.

You may be ready to dismiss this point of view, naïvely thinking, "I don't care what others think or say." Eventually when the steam of romantic love slowly dissipates from the relationship, you are more prone to care about what others think of you. It is my recommendation that you should pick a partner who is compatible with you in appearance.

If you end up choosing a partner who is not so compatible in physical appearance, brace yourself and know what to expect from society. Be prepared to handle the challenges. Prepare yourself with a good rationale of your choice. Not because you have to defend or explain your choice to the world, but to protect yourself and your relationship from the harshness of the world around you. If you stand firm and convinced of your rationale, you will navigate through life much more easily. People have no business in judging you, but they do. And eventually, it will affect you.

2. Examine Your Thoughts and Feelings:

Think about your environment in which you are now. Think about the environment that shaped you. Acknowledge how you feel about it. Think about your parents, your immediate family, your teachers, your friends, and your coworkers. Identify which one of the above individuals put a frown on your brow; then identify the reasons.

Are you comfortable with the feeling you are experiencing now digging through your memory lane? Or is there something that stands out as harsh and disturbing?

When I think of my growing years, I have many strong feelings. For example, my mother was very strict and harsh with us. She was very quick in pointing out our shortcomings and our mistakes in daily routine life. Then she would bring it up in front of everybody else in the family. (FYI, it was a joint family—my grandparents, my uncle and aunty and their four children, and my parents and the four of us.) We felt so insulted and worthless that we wanted to go hide somewhere. I am saying "we" because my mom did that to all of my siblings.

I did not appreciate her attitude; in fact, it bothered me a great deal. For more than twenty years after I got married and moved away, I still had dreams about my mom's toughness. I woke up at night bothered and stressed with dreams.

As I was experiencing my childhood and teen years, I constantly thought about my mom's toughness—her disciplinarian, marshal-like behavior—and made a resolution that I would treat my children with the utmost softness and affection that comes from a place of respect and love.

Even though I am very much like my mother in so many ways, yet because of my reaction to my mother's behavior, I managed to carefully shape my personality not-to-be like her in that respect. When I had the opportunity as an adult to have a conversation with my mom, she gave me her reasons why she did that. She admitted that's all she knew. She claimed that in her mind that was the best way to discipline children and prepare them for life.

Once I understood my mother's perspective, I was able to move on. I stopped having dreams that woke me up in the

middle of the night—sweating and angry. I guess I had successfully resolved my childhood issues with my mother.

Before I got married, as an adult, I was keenly aware that it was a good thing, and in fact it was an asset, to be gentle, respectful, and affectionate not only to my children to be, but to people at large. I freely share my asset/strength with the world around me.

With this awareness, I was able to highlight this part of my personality, and I benefitted. How? I consciously set a bar for myself not to ever deviate from that pleasant behavior. Habits that are positively received by society are branded with you. Do you see the benefit here? Practicing something on a conscious level is forged into habits. By recognizing and acknowledging your feelings and thoughts, you are highlighting your positive personality traits.

The person whose memory is associated with a pleasant smile on your face, there has to be a reason for it. Recognize those people who made you feel loved and appreciated. Is this person your parent, uncle, teacher, or a friend's mother? Go deeper down your memory lane and clarify to yourself what brings about that comfortable feeling.

Which of these people are very important to you and why? Think of your reaction to them; how do they impact your attitude? This will help you identify the people and circumstances that you liked. Perhaps you would like to build on that happiness in your future life. Perhaps you would like to emulate and intensify the positive personality traits of all those good people in your life.

3. What is Your Belief System?

By definition, "belief" refers to a psychological state in which a person holds to a premise, or an idea, that he or she discerns to be true. Belief is similar to knowledge, but it's differentiated by a level of stronger confidence and perhaps even of faith. It can also be defined as a person's justified true belief.

One could say that belief is, simply put, knowledge that has been proven true according to reason, plausibility, and evidence. Belief and knowledge are relative to the perception of one individual. Therefore, what- ever a person wants to believe will end up becoming their reality.

Your belief system is the very foundation of your being. Your belief system causes you to react to others' thoughts and actions. You develop conflict if what you experience with others doesn't match your belief system. That means your core belief system is different and you want people to understand you correctly. You are in total harmony when surrounded by people who are on the same page as you.

Again, your belief system grows as you experience life. You always anticipate conclusions as situations occur. If the results match what you anticipated, you develop faith in your judgment and in yourself. You will take yourself seriously. It relates to your self-esteem. You have to identify what matters to you and what does not. Are you in sync with your inner little voice called your "conscience"? Every time we do something when nobody is there to judge us, our conscience communicates with us by default. Whether you listen to that little voice or ignore it is your choice, but it is there.

Each of us has access to guidance if we would take the time to listen to it. However, this guidance system has roots deeply originating from our own conditioning system, our environment, and our package in its entirety.

Identify your core beliefs.

4 What Role does Religion and Traditions Play in Your Life?

One's relationship with their religion is very much like their relationship with their mother. You may not openly admit your complex feelings about her—but you know them to be true. One may feel a level of ownership about their mother, and thus say what they want to say about her. You have every right to feel however you feel about your mother. The relationship is very personal to you and to you alone. However, if someone else were to say negative things about her, it would be unacceptable and intolerable. The same can be said about religion if it is an important part of your life.

Pay close attention to the following dialogue as it will make that distinction clearer.

State to yourself what kind of ideal family you would want in your life. Imagine your ideal family and see who is in it. Do you see yourself being comfortable in a cross-racial, cultural, and ethnic family? Do you find yourself dating within your own kind of social order? You have to be perfectly at peace with what you want to deal with in your life. If you see too many concerns coming up, your belief system is on full alert and probably in your discomfort zone. Rearrange your ideal family in your head.

Does religion has a place in your belief system? Do you attend your church/temple routinely? Recall when you were growing up—was religion an integral part of your family?

Would you like to see your family unit going through the same rituals as you did growing up? Or you would like to raise your children without any religion? Why does it matter? You may or may not be religious. Your children will have to be raised in a certain way. Religion with most families is a way of life. Most of the things we do in our daily life originate from our religious faith.

Religious beliefs also fortify marital vows. Yet today fewer and fewer couples share a religious view of marriage as a covenant between a man and a woman before God. In fact, only 42 percent of young people consider it important to marry someone with the same religion. As a result, for many couples their wedding vows don't have the same force of commitment.

Your traditions, specifically your religion have a very special place in your heart just as your parents do. They all anchor you with roots; these may be good or bad is irrelevant. Now is the time to think through and figure out the role religion and traditions will play in your married life, before it is a problem down the road. Story # 3 in chapter five illustrates this point very clearly.

As a young adult, you may not be religious. Most of us are not regular church goers. But when you have children of your own, you feel responsible to give your family a value system and a belief system. Religion can begin to play a significant role and impact your life style.

If you and your spouse are coming from different religious backgrounds and you both are stuck in individual beliefs; what would you want your children to believe? If you already have a relationship with a person of a different faith, open up discussions now. This will help put you both on a clear path. Your future life will not suffer from undisclosed assumptions.

I am not implying that marriages between couples of different faiths are impossible to work-out. However, marriage is a lot of work and adding layers on it may complicate things.

It is a good idea to check with couples who come from different religious backgrounds. Talk about their experiences. Have a candid conversation with them. It will help pave the way for you. If this becomes a part of your conscious concerns, you will give a lot of weight to this subject while choosing your mate. You will share your vision with your spouse for the life with your children. If you are raised with religion all around your life's activities, you are bound to take it up in your children's life.

Are you a conscientious person? This is not a judgment on you; however, it is important to know. If you are a very conscientious person, you should be looking for someone as a life partner who also is conscientious. Otherwise, you would be miserable in your relationship. This is in direct relationship with your self-worth.

When subconscious mind and your conscious-self come to terms with each other, it allows you to execute plans and take action.

This will in turn propel your belief system and create confidence and guidance.

No matter how you see it, your belief system can be a real propeller in your life's happiness or it can block you. Make sure your belief system is not questioning the very fiber of your partner's behavior. If it does, it will be a road to hell. Be open minded and respectful in general. However, find a partner with a belief system based on similar values.

5. Examine the Role of Family in Your Own Life:

Examine the importance of certain relations in your future life. For example, what are your feelings and thoughts about your siblings and parents? What kind of role did your extended family play when you were growing up? Do you feel that involvement level was too much, perhaps overbearing and intrusive? If you don't know, talk to your family about it. You will be amazed to find out how different members were impacted by that intrusiveness. This will be an educational conversation.

In some cultures, especially Indian and Middle Eastern cultures, interference of the families can be so overbearing that a couple may feel totally powerless. The couple's happiness depends on the perception of the family—how the family views and accepts your partner. Make no assumptions. Be very clear to yourself about the kind of extended family you've got in your package. How will it affect your journey as a married person?

Examine the role of your parents and grandparents in your own life. Were you raised by both of your natural parents? Who else was involved during your growing years? Was it a stepparent? Some folks are raised by grandparents, while some grow up with a single parent or split their time with their mother and father and their respective families. Go down memory lane and bring up the feelings and thoughts you had as a child. What was good about the family environment that shaped you? What was your reaction then and now? What lessons did you learn from your experiences?

Coming to the point, if you had a loving and caring family, you will definitely want to give that same kind of rich experience to your children and your partner. If you suffered emotionally or in any other manner because you grew up in a not so desirable environment, the lesson learned should be that you will do your best and never give up trying to provide the best environment for your family. Your belief system might suggest contrary to what you want—a wishy-washy feeling about love, compassion, and steadiness. But know in your heart that if you want, you can strive to achieve a very favorable environment for your family.

People, who go through repeat marriages or relationships, carry with them so many unresolved issues. Same issues are then handed down to their children.

Thus you create a chain of bad "karma," and the damage is multigenerational.

Children grow up to become very much like their parents. All that they see, hear, and experience growing up, is ingrained in their subconscious mind.

As a result, that behavior becomes the norm for them, as they grow up to become adults.

Most people set their lives on auto pilot and thus driven by their subconscious behavior. They are so busy with being frustrated about their output and lack of results that they hardly think of the root cause of their disappointment. People quickly find faults with their partner and look for a quick relief by getting angry, argumentative or shutting off completely from the situation. They do not pause to look deeper within to find that changing their own behavior will positively affect their relationship.

The purpose of going through this mental diagnostic is to have a clear view of what your experiences taught you. Thus you will be aware of what behavior to repeat or avoid in your married life. In addition, you will also confront unresolved issues of your own which can help you move ahead with a crisp, clear focus and purpose.

Do you want to see your parents playing a very important role in your children's life? If the answer is yes, you have placed a valuable role for your parents and your family members in your future. If they are absent from yours and your children's life, it will make you unhappy. So if you want to highlight the importance of family in your married life, then you need to choose a partner who also believes in the role of parents just as you do.

6. Recognize Your Social Skills:

We get vibes from other people. Some vibes are good and comfortable, while others are bad vibes. Think about the situations or scenarios in your past experiences that caused good vibes and bad vibes. What role do these people play in your life? Are they important? The vibes you receive hint at general acceptance of your personality.

Are those people important to you? Is it your boss or a coworker or some family members or friends around whom you don't feel so good? Identify the root cause of your discomfort with them. Recognize the people who give you good vibes and vice versa. This will sharpen your awareness of different personality types. You will be able to choose your partner much more wisely.

If you meet a new crowd, notice how other people perceive you by just talking to you for a minute or so. If you have a friendly demeanor and you don't offend anybody, it means that you come across as a harmless person and can get along with most people in general. If you think that you do offend people easily, find out what needs to change. If you have a problem with your boss, analyze why so. Is it you or is it your boss who is unreasonably demanding? Would you like to fix it? Is it only you who is having a difficult time with the boss? If that is the case, look at your work habits and your work ethics in general and make amends.

Does it matter to you how others think and talk about you? If it does, you will try to correct the image. If it does not matter to you what others think of you, then you wouldn't care.

This is again not a judgment call. However, it is important to know. If you are a very conscientious person, you will be looking for someone as a life partner who also is conscientious. Otherwise, you would be miserable. Are you true to your own word, meaning do you follow through with your commitments? This is in direct relationship with your self-worth and being conscientious.

7. Are You Confident?

Do you believe in yourself? Whether you do or you don't depends where you are in your life. As a young student, maybe in high school, it is hard to answer this question. You are still growing, learning, and testing your self-knowledge. If you are at a stage where you have been wheeling and dealing in life for a while, then you are in a position to answer this question.

This part of self-knowledge is extremely important as it also directly relates to your inner being and your overall comfort level with yourself. You are bound to be on firm footing if you believe in yourself, no matter what you are doing in life.

8. Do You Want to be Married?

Ask this question of yourself. Getting married creates a chain of responsibilities. Are you up for it? "Falling in love" is not enough as stand-alone reason. How is this relationship different from others that did not work out? Is there a child on the way? Get in touch with your own sexuality. Check out all the relationships that you had. Answer to yourself why this one feels right.

Getting married is not a destination.

Ask yourself if you want children. I know a friend who helped his parents raise his siblings. He had no desire to have children of his own. He got married and his wife wanted children. He divorced her.

Think about your feelings if you don't happen to have children. Can you deal with it? You can take a little flight with your imagination to answer this question clearly. Imagine the environment in which you would like to raise them. Your mind will rush through your own childhood memories and determine a path for you. Create and lay out your idea of a perfect family.

The responsibility of having a family can be grueling at times. Make yourself conscious of the challenges ahead and make sure that you are okay dealing with life's tough situations as they present themselves. After all, the purpose of this exercise is to prepare you mentally to take the right road.

9.   Are You Fiscally Responsible?

If you know how to budget and then stick to it, you are fiscally responsible. Money is a limited commodity for a huge majority of us. One has to prioritize family needs and make a lot of personal sacrifices. If your finances are in a mess, you lose a lot of leverage in life. Can you afford your lifestyle? If not, what steps will you take to improve your financial situation?

Do you need another income to support the lifestyle you currently have and wish to have in the future?

Think how crucial it is for you to have a partner who is not crazy about shopping senselessly. Give it all serious thought so that you can pick a partner who is not a huge drain on your finances but someone who is in alignment with you in fiscal responsibilities.

Studies have shown that disagreements about money are one of the leading causes of marital breakdown. Compromise is perhaps the most important ingredient for a successful union, especially when it comes to financial matters.

But what happens when the two parties in a marriage have vastly different money beliefs and practices? How can they arrive at a workable arrangement when they have opposite money personalities?

So be mindful that your future partner needs to be in tune with you on money matters.

10.   Can You Think Outside The Box?

This topic refers to a person's ability to look for new and creative ways of problem solving and looking at things from a fresh perspective. Some people only like to apply what they already know. They will perform an activity just the way they learned it from their parents, teachers, or guides. If anybody offers a different approach, they get very upset. On the other hand, some people look for fresh new ideas for everything they do.

There is always more than one option to approach a problem. Do you know about the parachute analogy? The mind works only if it is open—just like a parachute.

Be mindful of which one of these two ideologies you subscribe to. As you look for a partner, bear in mind what your partner brings to the table and ask yourself if you can deal with it.

Understand Your Total Package

After analyzing your health, fitness, and physical appearance (to include your mannerisms, the way you dress, if you are confident, your self-esteem, etc.), you should create a bar for yourself. You should evaluate yourself. Find out what you like about other people's appearance— people that appeal to you; people that you think look good, healthy, and attractive. Then pick up the positive notes and compare it to your own physique. Consciously work on making the changes where you deem necessary, and in no time, you will achieve it.

There is nothing we cannot change. Some things are easier than others. I knew I had bad posture sitting down. For forty-five years of my life, I did not do anything about it. I just hated myself for doing so. One day, I talked to my physical trainer at the gym about my concern. He showed me a couple of exercises and told me how to always engage different muscles of my abdomen; believe it or not, it corrected my problem.

If your health is not in the best of shape, you should be ready to tackle this issue head-on. Your health is the leading component in the quiz of life. A lot of possibilities rest on it. Do what you can to fix it. It will only make you better. It will give you confidence.

After setting some goals in this arena, move on to figure out your value and belief system. Spell it out for yourself. Once confronted with this knowledge, you will become very mindful of the differences in individu- als, cultures, and races. Your mind will be open to new horizons. This knowledge will address the depth, the sensitivity, the understanding, and the deeper sense of the human psyche within you. You will come to know your own character.

Confront your belief system. As an adult, you will be able to know what beliefs are knowledge-based and what beliefs are fear and emotion-based.

You have unconsciously developed your belief system so far—we all do. It's time to put it in perspective and make some changes.

Next, you should spell out the makeup of your ideal family. Assign the role of parents, grandparents, siblings, friends, and teachers. Assign a value to religion in your family's life.

Check your career status—are you comfortable in this zone? Otherwise, look for ways to enhance your capabilities. Do you need more education or professional training? Set your long and short-term goals.

Now look at your personality traits. Check your daily routine. Is it in alignment with your work, fitness, and social life? Take a look at your personal habits like eating and cleanliness. Write down if you need some fine-tuning.

Take a look at your personal attitude. Are you happy, angry, or stressed in general? Find out the root cause. If it makes you genuinely happy without damaging anybody or anything, great! Keep it up! If you experience stress or anguish most of the time, find out the source. Work on making things better.

Take a look at your temperament. Do you have so much endurance that people can walk over you without upsetting you? Or are you a person with a short fuse? Both scenarios are not healthy. You should check for balance. It pays to tame your anger; it pays to stand up for what is right.

Check on your ego. Ego is not a bad thing to have. We all have it to varying degrees. If your ego propels you to do good things and enhances your life in a positive way, it is a wonderful asset. Watch out if your ego is so big that it enslaves your mind; it can become a disease. Keep yourself grounded with the realities of the self. If you don't, you will lose your ground; you will forget your identity; you will lose your balance in life. Keep your ego in check.

Knowledge of your own package will help you move towards what you need for your future success and happiness. Now you can dream up big things and achieve them all.

◆————◆————◆

Your Thoughts:

1. How do you describe yourself:
   • Physical Appearance
   • Health
   • Education/Career
   • Hobbies
   • Temperament

2. Describe your family:
   • Assess your relationship with your parents and siblings

3. Who is your mentor?
   • Describe why and what makes that person qualify as your mentor
   • Describe your mentor's temperament

4. What is your opinion of the place of religion in life?
   • What is your view of your own religion?
   • What is your view of other cultures?
   • What is your view of the importance of traditions?

5. Describe the traditions of your family:
    *   What traditions would you like to uphold?
    *   If you didn't have any, but you are aware of traditions that other folks have, would you like to take up those traditions?

6. Describe your ideal self.
7. Describe your ideal mate.
8. Create a to-do list based on how you can improve your package.

CHAPTER NINE

ENVISION YOUR FUTURE

You can build a compelling future that is so appealing that it becomes everything you want to live for. How do you want to be feeling about yourself a year from now? And do you think there is a limit to how far you can go? No, there isn't.

The dreams you envision in your future with a sense of opened possibility not only fill you up with great excitement, but they also imprint the believability to create it. The better your dreams are, the more compelling your life will become! The more glorious you envision your future to be, the more it will propel you to create it.

That's why it is so useful to envision a future that drives you. It's about finding out what's most important to you. In order to create it easily, use your focus, intent, and action.

The world's greatest leaders, speakers, and celebrities all have one thing in common. They have unshakable intent, and they take action toward their dreams and desires. Despite what anyone else thinks, and no matter what obstacles get in their way, they carve their way through.

You use your intent to have fun at a party. You go to a classroom with the intent to gain knowledge. You can use this same intent and action that you use every day to build your self-esteem and confidence beyond measure by improving upon your personality, education, career, and all that you want.

Remember, the most outrageous castles (projects) are erected in someone's dreams first; the tradesmen offer technical support to put foundations underneath. When you start taking a course at college, you know what you want out of that class. If you are shooting for a degree, you carefully select courses that will count toward the achievement of a degree. Marriage and married life is no different. So dream your future.

Create some excitement in life.

Envision your life as a married person. Think in detail what kind of life partner you want. What are the minimum assets (qualities) that person should bring to the table? What kind of lifestyle will suit you? How much income will you need to support that lifestyle? Don't just stop here. Where would you like to live with your family? Where would you like your children to go to school? When and how would you like to retire? What kind of social status would you want? What do you want people to say about you when you die? Now, having the end results in mind, you can create a grand vision. Believe it or not, you will live your vision if you accept that possibility.

Your dream will create intention, action, and direction. You need to be sincere about your dream. You will recognize opportunities knocking when they match up with your dream. Your life will be full of excitement. You will see purpose. You still will have challenges, but they will be challenges only, not show-stoppers.

Remember, we learn and grow all life-long; Growing means tweaking our lifestyle to meet our goals or challenges that life presents to us from time to time. It means changing personal habits or better equipping with the tools of the trade to give ourselves better opportunities to enjoy life.

CHAPTER TEN

FIND A COMPATIBLE PARTNER

In the previous chapters, you answered questions to yourself that will lead you to imagine your future. Hopefully, that led you to find out who you are and what kind of life you would like to have. This chapter deals with matching an ideal mate who will complement you and be an asset to your future life. The essence of this chapter is what to look for and what to avoid while searching for a compatible spouse.

You must realize that **nobody is perfect**. Everybody is a package of some good and some not so good. Growing up, you kind of know who you want to be like or who your hero is. Go down your memory lane and confront your impressions. How do your mom and dad fit in the framework of your liking and disliking? Do you like everything about them? Did you want to be exactly like your parents when you grew up? I guess in some ways we like to be like our family. Most of us would like to be better providers or not so strict with our children or much more involved with our children in school and after-school activities.

Nonetheless, while growing up, all of us form opinions of people who interact in our little world.

You identify heroes and villains within the makeup of your family. Your world as a child will play a big role in forming your view of your future life.

Love and harmony can only prevail if a couple is dancing to the same tune.

So let's explore what matters to you. What should you be concerned about? The real question is how you should determine if a person is compatible with you or not.

You must figure what is important to you. Is it the appearance of a person? Is it the social status? Is it how much money the other person can bring to the table? Are you looking for a good basic human being? What matters to you most? What is big stuff and small stuff for you? What is big stuff for one person may be small stuff for another and vice versa. You have to figure it out on your own what is important to you.

What is "big stuff"? It stems from your belief system. Your belief system depends on how and where you were raised and where you are in life today. If you grew up with strong traditions, where social sanctions had a strong role, you will be internally aware and practice caution with everything you do. Religion, culture, and ethnicity might be "big stuff" for you.

If you are someone who was born and brought up in a cosmopolitan type atmosphere, you have been exposed to a variety of cultures and beliefs. Go down a generation or two. What was your home atmosphere like? Think in terms of acceptance of individual freedom, individual views, discipline and parental control, general fairness, fights and arguments and how they were settled, place of religion and traditions, education, health and happiness, and so forth.

Do you appreciate and accept the individual differences without being too critical? Are you comfortable with different viewpoints and lifestyles? Do you have friends from all walks of life? Then for you, "big stuff" may or may not include culture, religion, and ethnicity. So while looking for a mate, you may be able to recognize as "big stuff" which is more of personal nature to include personality traits, social and vocational skills, and so forth.

The other part to the equation of "big stuff" relates to where you are in life today. Are you marrying more or less for companionship, or do you want to have and raise children in your marriage? Are you an exceptionally wealthy person and looking for a trophy spouse? Or do you have to live and deal with middle and working-class society? Based on where you are in life, big stuff and small stuff will have different meanings for you. You and only you have to figure it out.

This book is written to promote a stable and balanced family life. Obviously, the goal is to marry once and have it right the first time around. The factors that dictate compatibility are universally applicable. Understanding and acceptance of these guiding factors will help you eliminate a lot of problems from your married life.

Marriage may be between two people; the strength of that marriage, however, is based largely on acceptance and approval of families.

How does the other person's race, religion, and level of education compare to your own? Are there any indicators that make you even a tiny bit uncomfortable and concerned? These are big factors that will play a huge role in how you develop your relationship with your future spouse.

Don't just blow it off. If these factors match your own profile, you've got a broad basis covered.

The 80 Percent Rule:

Simply put, you do not have to have exactly the same or similar aptitudes and skills to be compatible as a couple. While exploring your profile, focus on the "big stuff." If you two are compatible 80 percent on the big stuff that matters to you, you just purchased a warranty for a great relationship. Little stuff will have to find adjustments.

No two people are exactly alike, not even brothers and sisters. Living in a family, everybody has to make some concessions to accommodate others. We fight, we argue, but we forgive and forget. We make mistakes and we learn from it. Doing so, we develop a belief system, a value system.

Our belief system guides us in making everyday choices—choices that develop into habits and then into a lifestyle. For example, if you grow up believing that receiving an education is not a choice but a must, you will not ponder on the idea if you should get up and be on time to catch your school bus. Routinely, you will do just that. Even though you are tempted to sleep a little longer, you know better. Your family advocates that going to school is a non-negotiable part of your everyday life.

All other associated activities like getting up at a certain time, taking a shower in the morning, dressing up for school, making your bed before you leave, and eating breakfast becomes a routine for you. Or doing all these activities in a certain manner becomes your second nature. They become **your** habits. Good or bad is not a question. You are familiar with that pattern.

If it worked well enough for you, you will remember it when you are raising your children. All that you experienced in your childhood will be called to your memory. You might have to tweak that routine to make it work better in your current environment, but it has become part of your belief system that receiving education is a must and non-negotiable.

Take the other side of the same belief that schooling is not necessary. All your activities will shift. You may not have to do any of the activities associated with going to school every day. Whatever you do becomes your routine. Thus, you develop your habits and your lifestyle.

Other examples of developing a belief system could be going to church every Sunday; or cleaning up your room, your house, and your surroundings; or your eating habits, such as eating at proper times and eating nutritious foods and or vice versa. It becomes part of you and part of your lifestyle.

Your belief system changes as you grow. Sticking with the same example, as an adult you realize that going to school every day was not a bad idea. In fact, it was a great thing to do. Now you would want all your loved ones to avail themselves of the opportunity to receive an education. That is now a part of your belief system.

What is Your Value System?

Your value system is a bar, a level against which you check your belief system and your minimum performance in daily life. You do it by default. Nobody enforces it upon you. It is your expectation of yourself. If your performance is not up to your own bar, it makes you uncomfortable.

If you are attracted to someone and thinking about marrying that person, there has got to be some foundation to that—perhaps physical attraction and some working chemistry just to start off. What else is there? How well you do know that person? Initial attraction wears off very quickly. You cannot expect to have a lifelong relationship based on just romantic love. After all, as partners, you are products of different environ- ments. Two partners are bound to be different.

The more similarities you have, the less friction you will have in the journey of your married life. It is okay if you find that the two of you are different on many fronts. Knowing what you have in the package, you will be better prepared to handle it along the way. If you don't give yourself the opportunity to know each other now and communicate your thoughts and feelings, your life will be consumed with unsubstantiated expectations that are bound to get you down sooner or later.

Are You Compatible?

Check out the following **five** broad-based categories. After recognizing your "big stuff," you will very well know how to apply your knowledge of the self to find the most compatible partner for a long and beautiful journey of marital bliss.

1. Personality Compatibility:

What's inside a person is the most important factor because that is always going to be there. Find out what personality types you are mostly attracted to. Some people enjoy a great sense of humor; others may look for certain spiritual values and belief system. Some are sports fanatics or music lovers or obsessed with some other hobby that you may not care for. Many people are very reserved. They think a lot and speak very carefully. Others might find this trait boring.

It is okay to be interested in different things. Remember, as a couple the more things you do joyfully together, the better it is. As a couple, you would want to slowly give up things that don't interest both of you. You may like theatre and your friend totally may not care for it. He may be willing to go with you to such events. But watch out for little signals—for example, he has been yawning the whole time or he has been looking at his watch. So you get it—he is not into theatre. Ask yourself if you are a performer or part of the passionate audience. How often you expect to go to the theatre each month in your future life? Will you have time to support your hobby of going to such performances once you have a family? How would it affect you? Are you willing to go to the sports events your friend so passionately cares about? If this is all casual and both of you are not fixated about it, you both will show respect to each other's liking and disliking and mutually, and you will decide how big of a deal it is for you and your partner. Then you will determine if it is big stuff for you or not.

You both have to have the mindset to understand the complexity of the relationship and be willing to make sacrifices. Therefore, the more interests you have in common, the less sacrifice you will have to make.

Some people fall for just looks or physical attraction. Hormonal rage could be rightfully blamed. They become so oblivious to the sharp contrasts they have. In fact, they ignore the existence of it. After marriage, when they have each other 24-7, then other factors hit them as if a tennis ball hit them between the eyes. They find themselves dumbstruck. What they thought they loved so much is now meaningless. They are not happy campers.

When bigger and more important issues are trivialized or shoved under the rug, and never get attended to; the marriage will not have a strong foundation to build your life together. You will find yourself derailed very quickly.

One must recognize the differences, the likes and the dislikes of each other's everyday routine lifestyle. You both must appreciate and respect the importance of it.

For example, let's say that you are a tea drinker; you do not even touch alcohol. You don't want to be with a person who is heavily into drinking. What kind of behavior changes does his/her drinking bring about?

What causes him/her to drink? These are important questions. More importantly, you must evaluate if you have the courage, strength, and willingness to deal with the issues that are not in tune with your personality.

If you are very different in many respects and still like each other a lot, it is still fine. There is nothing to be really alarmed about. You need to understand your partner's behavior from their perspective. You need to understand the differences, accept them, and respect them. Take time to get to know your partner's true nature.

2.   Communication Compatibility:

Are you and your sweetheart on the same page in terms of communication? See if your conversations flow and if they are enjoyable for both of you.

If you butt heads frequently, find out what causes it. Is it about some silly stuff or about everything? If you two find yourselves bickering all the time, you need to figure out now if this should be tolerated. If one of you just caves in and the other person is okay with that, then you have potential "control" issues. This is rated as "big stuff."

On some subjects, one person could have a better knowledge than their counterpart. It is of course okay to yield. If this is about establishing supremacy in every conversation, you should be concerned. You are in great danger of getting into a potentially abusive relationship.

When you're in love, you might think you have the best conversations, when really one of you is doing all the talking. While you are getting to know each other, keep conversations real and fun. Can you read each other and see if you both are seriously taking the conversation to a deeper level so that you can understand each other's point of view? Some people are not very verbal, which is okay. How the verbal and nonverbal communication affects each other makes a difference.

Is one of you being sarcastic or going into ridicule mode often? Watch out for the symptoms. It shows lack of respect. Lack of respect means that you do not give proper value to the others' point of view. Can you talk and listen with care, respect, and proper appreciation? Are you easily admitting when you are wrong, or do you find yourself being defensive instead?

A good relationship does not mean that you don't argue. It means you are disagreeing, gracefully and respectfully. Your tone of voice does not change to an angry level. If one person behaves like this, does the other person have the ability to calm it down and make it clear that it wasn't meant to be personal? Can you then laugh about it? Can you then hug each other, or do you have to change the subject and never bring it up again, or possibly the silent treatment takes over for days?

If the latter condition persists, you can expect screaming, door slamming, and running out of the house as frequent behavior as life happens.

Can you deal with it? Can your family deal with it? Would you want your children to grow up in an environment that is bitter and negative? That is "big stuff."

3.   Social/Ethnic/Religious Compatibility:

We live in an immigrant society in the United States of America. Chances are that you are exposed to a variety of cultures. You may like somebody from a different ethnic and cultural background. Remember as I said earlier that the more things you have in common, the less challenge you will have in your married life.

Long-lived marriages are not only between a man and a wife; it seeks to summon support from immediate family-members.

It matters especially if you are in the early years of life and if you wish to have children together. If families are compatible in social status, value and belief system, and economic background, then life runs quite smoothly. If there are huge differences in the outlook of your families, every get-together becomes a nightmare. If your families live far apart, you don't worry about it as much.

You are a product of your environment.

So naturally, you will choose someone with similar or tolerably-different backgrounds.

If one family is a total slob and the other one is quite sophisticated, you will encounter problem after problem. No matter how bad your family is, you cannot tolerate other people telling you so. No matter how true it is and even if you yourself know it deep-down, but coming from somebody else might be totally intolerable.

If you ignore family-compatibility, then both of you will have to be super-sensitive and supportive of each other without losing the balance in your relationship.

Be aware of cultural and ethnic differences in the background of your families.

If you two come from two different religious faiths, two different ethnic groups, two different languages, then imagine your birthdays and anniversaries when both sides of your families have to be together. What if your families are totally unappreciative of each other's way of life? If you two come from the same traditions, you will very naturally walk into each other's lives and just mingle and enjoy life.

Unless you talk about this stuff up front and build realistic expectations, your relationship will be in trouble even before you know it.

How about the language barrier? I have seen families where

English is not the first language for one of the two families. After a few minutes of formal dialogue, people begin to start talking, laughing, and joking in their own language. If you are a guest among a group of people who do not speak or understand your language, you will soon find yourself embarrassed, lonely, and out of place. You will find the environment suffocating. This will restrict your visits to the family affairs and will affect your relationship with your spouse.

Religious-beliefs is another area of huge concern. Whether or not you are religious now, it is going to matter to you once you have children. If one of you has deep-rooted religious beliefs, if they are not the same as your counterpart's beliefs, one of two things will happen. You could zip your lips for rest of your life and exist as a non-person. Or you could find yourself constantly combating and trying hard to protect your faith and belief system. Choose what you like, but be aware of the upcoming challenges if you are marrying into a different faith.

Check out story #3 in part one of this book where Liz and Salim's marriage could not survive as Salim turned out to be very religious after they had a child. This may sound silly, but you must think through and accept each other's families, culture, and religious beliefs. Have realistic expectations and have a plan to deal with what comes with the package. Your love and commitment can still make it work. Just be aware. **It's "big stuff."**

4.   Financial Compatibility:

Imagine that you are very conservative with your money and you are a hard-working individual with a reasonable income. If you marry somebody who must have frequent visits to spas, expensive restaurants, and shopping malls or other expensive hobbies and does not understand priorities in spending, how long can you hold your peace?

You must understand how you set your priorities managing money. This will impact you and your marriage if your other half holds money managing beliefs that are diametrically opposite to yours. Money is a scarce commodity for most of us. Every family has different priorities spending money. I come across many folks in my real estate business that make a lot of money but their credit is messed up. Their finances are in disarray. I notice that it creates a lot of tension among spouses.

Old habits die hard. Be watchful. If you are entering into a marriage relationship, financial responsibility is the single biggest issue that can put a serious strain on a relationship. Unless you are a billionaire and you have money to burn, you must sense each other's priorities in spending habits and be candid enough to tell each other how serious it is. Come to terms as to how to use or invest funds. Find out about each other's frivolities and talk about the importance of handling money responsibly.

5. Compatibility in Level of Education:

In today's world, women and men are equally educated and generally account for dual-career families. The burden to provide for the family is no longer limited to being a man's job. Formal education not only prepares us for formal career paths, but it molds and shapes our consciousness. Education adds to status— and who does not love status?

Therefore, it is natural to be compatible in the field of education. It does not mean that a PhD must marry a person with a similar degree. It simply means that we should have a good comprehension of each other's field of expertise. We should understand the expectations and value related to each other's career.

It is not advisable to have one person of high academic profile while the partner is totally illiterate or just pretty. A skin-deep beauty does not compensate for maturity, wisdom, or sophistication that comes from all areas of development of one's personality.

No matter how careful we are, never forget that we are still human beings. In some silly moments, we all can be swayed into a moment of irrational competition. We might end up bruising our relationship in an attempt to show our superiority. It is very common to see power abuse when one partner is not able to contribute to the family income. With competitive career training (education), this potential abuse can be avoided.

It is a common occurrence in social environments when couples introduce their partners to their friends or peers; people assign a value to each person based on their careers, and an expectation of level of conversation is established naturally. Whenever there are inequities present, it leads to an inferiority complex and therefore leads to embarrassments. The tension thus created leads to tip the scale to imbalance.

Know what kind of social environments you would like to walk in. Your partner should be a well-rounded individual who can complement your status. Your partner should be able to carry on a conversation without being generally intimidated or humiliated. It does not matter what kind of field you or your partner are in.

If you and your partner cannot present yourselves as a great team in the outer world, you will end up developing your independent social safe escapes. Your "together" time will be lost. You will grow apart. For a balanced and happy marriage, you should be proud to be with each other. You should be able to speak highly of each other with your heads held high. This will help you to grow together happily ever after. This is "big stuff."

All the above discussion contributes to creating your value system. Your value system gives direction to your future. If you are compatible in all these major fields of life, you've got it made. As long as you like each other, your work is reduced to handling little things in your daily routine, and there is nothing to be concerned about. Just make sure that you assign the proper value to the little differences and do not overreact; you should be respectful when you argue your point. Accept each other's shortcomings. Complement and accentuate what is positive and strong about one another and learn to cash in on it jointly.

PART THREE

THE MARRIAGE CODE

A marital relationship is like a ship on the ocean, which at all times must know its' destination and its' position. Most marriages that take a fall are like a lost ship—whose radar is not in place; it goes wherever the winds take it, and lasts as long as it does; then falls apart.

CHAPTER ELEVEN

CREATE A "MISSION-IN-MARRIAGE" STATEMENT

For all organizations, a mission statement tells the world what is the spirit and guiding light of the organization that will keep it in check throughout its life. A mission statement is permanent even though policies and procedures keep changing to run the organization at its optimum level. A mission statement keeps the organizers grounded and properly rooted in its mission.

A "mission-in-marriage" statement is no different. It's highly recommended to have one to cope with the ever-changing world and to help you stay in focus to successfully handle the ship of your marriage.

Once you and your beloved decided to tie the knot, you need a business plan, and every good business plan has a mission statement. Hopefully, if you are reading this, you have already determined who you want to go into business with. You have made sure that you have similar business philosophies (ideas about marriage), and you know with certainty that your business partner is reliable and honest and is someone you can work with to achieve your goals.

Let's consider first of all that nothing is set in stone. A good business plan must allow for flexibility. Think of a business plan as a road map. It's simply a tool to show you where you are going and how you intend to get there. So you have chosen your BP (business partner) and you're ready to begin planning. The obvious goal of your business is for the two of you to have happy and fulfilling lives through your marriage to one another. However, flexibility is of utmost importance. Even though roles should be established, the other partner must be flexible enough to fill in as needed.

In establishing the roles, a successful business will draw upon the expertise of its partners. Know beforehand who is better at certain tasks, such as budgeting and balancing the checkbook, generating income, lawn care and housekeeping, personnel training like helping the kids with their homework (though that may come later), and so on. Many of these duties will be shared, and certainly all of them should be discussed frequently with the other partner so that should the need arise for them to step into your territory, the transition will be smooth.

With roles established, every good business needs a good mission statement. So how do you create a mission statement for your marriage? Simple! Focus on what you want your marriage to do and be, and then focus on the values and principles in which the doing or being are based.

My mission-in-marriage statement:

"To love, live, and grow old together, having a peaceful environment, supporting each other, sacrificing for each other, leaving a legacy of 'unconditional love and respect' for our children."

The irony is that our mission statement came in twenty years later. However, it's never too late to do the right thing.

Once you have your mission statement for your marriage, learn it. Keep it in focus. Let others know what your mission statement says. Sharing it with friends and family will only serve to strengthen your resolve to follow it daily.

A marital relationship is like a ship on the ocean, which at all times must know its destination and its position. Most marriages that take a fall are like a lost ship whose radar is not in place; it goes wherever the winds take it and lasts as long as it does and then falls apart.

A marriage's radar or its' guiding light is its mission-in-marriage statement that is backed with a carefully crafted and shared vision—a joint mission statement.

A joint mission statement is your vision for life; It is a mutual consent to support and promote each other's individuality while leading life hand in hand.

How do you arrive at a blueprint that makes sense to both of you? Start with your individual mission statement in life. Make a list of your wants, needs, and dreams of your life. Include what you want, academically, professionally, financially, socially, and personally in life.

All these wants and needs are interconnected, and you are aware of them consciously or unconsciously. By writing, you are bringing them under your radar—under your conscious focus. This exercise should help you carve out your wants, needs, and your goals in your life. Start out with your personal mission statement. You must think through the following:

- Position yourself where you stand on the canvas of your life today. Think about people around you who have importance to you—your family, friends, teachers, and religious leaders. Define the importance of their respective roles in your life.
- Think about your personal health. Are you sat- isfied with it? See if you need to pay attention to your nutrition or exercise. Do you have any restrictive handicaps? See to it that everything is what it can be and should be.
- See yourself in a marriage relationship and describe your ideal mate.
- Do you want children in your life? If so, think about the lifestyle or environment you would like to provide for them.

- Think about the role of mother, father, grand-parents, church, and school in the life of your family.
- Think about where you are academically or professionally. What else do you wish to do to improve? Give yourself a timeline by which you wish to achieve your goals.
- Check on the status of your finances. Are you happy with your status? If not, what steps can you take to reach your desired position?
- Think about places you want to visit and vacations you wish to take.
- Think about if you wish to do any charity work. Give it a check where, when, and how you wish to be involved.
- Is there anything else you wish to include in your list? Do so.

Should you write down your mission statement/wish list/blueprint? The answer is yes! Writing it out forces you to dig deep in your inner desires and bring them to the surface. Once you acknowledge something that you really would like to have, you will strive to get it. This is a good idea to make this a project for the year-end and keep a score of your progress. After writing it out in detail, keep tweaking and constantly prioritizing your list.

When you meet that special someone, pull out the list you prepared as your personal mission statement. See how that special someone adds value to your mission in life. Compare him/her against your checklist. You will have a happy union if you both bring positive things to the table, meaning your mission statements match on "big stuff" in life. Apply the 80 percent rule. Before you get married, share your list with your partner. Explain why each item is on the list and how important it is to you in life. Understand and appreciate your partner's mission. If your partner has not created a list, ask and encourage your mate to develop a wish list.

Prepare a Joint Mission Statement:

The idea of creating a joint mission statement has a two-fold benefit. One, by sharing your vision you are creating respect and appreciation for each other's wishes and dreams. Secondly, let this mission statement guide you in life so that whenever you find yourself derailed, you can come back to it. Therefore, if it is in writing, it becomes a very important living document for life.

When creating the joint wish list, be aware that you cannot foresee all situations and scenarios of your life.

Therefore, you cannot plan for your entire life. You can have a shared understanding and acceptance thereof. This is a living document. It will need tweaking. It will need additions from time to time. It is more like a constitution that provides understanding of purpose, clarity, and direction in life. You will have to prioritize your to-do list based on what life throws at you from time to time.

Put both lists side by side. Make sure you give due preference to each other's wants and needs. When preparing a joint mission statement, be very sure to keep a balance. Try to incorporate most from both lists. Do not run in competition. Do not think that in order for one to win the other must lose. Think what things take priority in your married life that helps to enhance your joint venture. "Family first, me later" should be the motto.

Once you are married, take five years at a time. See what both of you wish to accomplish in the first five years of your married life. Talk about your finances. See what you can afford to do. If a child is born, think about how your schedules will adjust to accommodate the baby. Do you both need to work? If you both feel that your careers are of equal importance, which one will make the most sacrifices or put their career on hold in the child-rearing period?

Kamini and Sam, married for five years, lack a joint mission statement. Here is their story as told by the wife:

"Sam asked me to marry him after a six-month-long head-over-heels courtship. He is a salesman for a drug company. He is also a painter. He has a degree in fine arts, and he taught fine arts in a university in Germany.

I loved what he did. I never asked what kind of money he was earning. [Kamini is a translator for the court. She enjoys her tedious work and the hours that go with it. She earns decent money.]

We had two children back-to-back. Sam was away at the time of birth of our first child. He had an exhibit scheduled in Germany. He did not want to get out of it. I hated going to the hospital by myself. I hated coming home with the baby with no one to greet us. I knew Sam had to work a lot and could not be disturbed, but his lack of understanding to share the responsibility of a baby and no consideration to my career makes me so mad. He does not even say that I should not worry about money, that he will provide for me and our baby. We don't have a joint account. I have to work to pay for our necessities. The babysitter is reliable, but that's not how I imagined my life. Then the second baby came.

"I thought Sam would pay attention as our family needs are changing. But he seems rather distant and lost in his own world. He goes to his regular work, and whenever he is home, he spends time working on his paintings. It seems like he has no responsibility toward our children. He comes out of his studio whenever he is tired. He plays with the kids at his leisure. I put the kids to bed. I wake up at night to attend to them. Then I take work to my bedroom. And Sam has the gall to tell me that I ignore his needs; that I am too wrapped up in the kids." Had Sam and Kamini talked about their life as a married couple before jumping into marriage heads down, I am pretty sure that the consequences could be different. They have no clue what is expected of each other.

Describe Your Mission Statement in Life:

List your goals for the next five to ten years in the following fields. If you have very long-range vision, feel free to include long-term goals here as well.

Your mission statement:

Health
Education/career
Finances
Marriage
Family/children
Role of immediate family in your life
Role of religion in your family's life
Role of your friends in your family's life
Place of your hobbies in your family life
Your liabilities/obligations towards your family
Other fields of interest, if any

Your partner's mission statement:

Health Education/career Finances Marriage Family/children
Role of immediate family in your life Role of religion in your family's life Role of your friends in your family's life
Place of your hobbies in your family life
Your liabilities/obligations towards your family Other fields of interest, if any

Now create a joint mission-in-marriage statement, which is more like a preamble to your life's blueprint. Your joint mission statement is your to-do list, or a wish list, that keeps your goals and their timings aligned with your long-term vision, purpose, and accomplishments. Merge the two individual statements and then prioritize. Now you have a blueprint for life. Now all you have to do is to combine your personal habits and your social skills to execute your blueprint in life.

A word of caution:

If you find yourself in a relationship and you are not married yet, this is the time to evaluate if you should proceed with it or withdraw from it. After going through all the foregoing chapters, your thoughts should be crisp and clear at this juncture and you should be able to see the writing on the wall. If you are in a good relationship then go ahead and read through the following chapters. Start out a great journey rooted in principles as called for in the following chapters.

If you find your relationship to be stressful, find out why? If the stress stems from some core issues that are related to your belief system, you better take a break from your current relationship. You deserve happiness and a very fulfilling relationship. If you are not understood and respected now, you will be rolling down the wrong alley. Your baggage will get heavier and heavier. It will be that much harder and longer to heal. So get out of this relationship right now. Suck up the pain right now and prepare yourself for the right relationship.

If you just got married and now realize that you have made the wrong choice; it is time to rethink what you got yourself into. If you married someone or forced into marrying someone, who you realize is totally wrong for you, think and think hard. See if you can find any positives that can connect two of you. Is that person worthy of you? Is he/she compatible with you? Is that person making you feel worthless? Don't think you can change the person, because it never happens. If you want to make peace in your life, you must accept that individual.

If two of your belief systems are running on totally different frequencies, your life is going to be an uphill battle and you will attract depression and misery. Before you set out to have children in such a marriage, you better get out of it as quickly as you possibly can. Think of it as a bad dream and shake it off. **Do not** prolong it.

Marriages may start out to be happy unions and slowly simmer into less satisfying as you start to settle down. This is a natural progression in any relationship. This is not a reason to think negatively of your marriage or your spouse. You both are settling into changing roles. You both are new to changing obligations, therefore, you both will misjudge and misinterpret your inter personal relationship. You need to adjust your paradigm. Look beyond the obvious and weed out the source of confusion. It is time for a new understanding. Your marriage can be very wholesome. You must stay focused on your mission-in-marriage and then your marriage will rock. You must have faith in each other and your marriage.

The Code for a Happy "Ever-After"

- *Thou shalt prepare a mission-in-marriage statement.*
- *Thou shalt love and respect each other and thy respective families.*
- *Thou shalt not be a hard-liner.*
- *Thou shalt recognize "compromise" as a virtue.*
- *Thou shalt understand your spouse's perspective first.*
- *Thou shalt accept one another for who you are.*
- *Thou shalt adopt a win-win, not a win-lose attitude.*
- *Thou shalt highlight each other's strengths, not shortcomings.*
- *Thou shalt never allow harsh words to escape thy lips.*
- *Thou shalt read these commandments when in doubt.*

Let the Code for a Happy "Ever- After" be your guide. Understand the importance of these statements. This should be your daily "mantra," and you should follow this code religiously. While both of you respect your mission-in-marriage that you co-created; the code will enable you to enjoy your grand vision of your life.

These statements stem from solemn principles that are discussed in the following chapters. Once you understand the strength behind the code, you will want to adopt it.

It will strengthen the value and belief system of your nuclear family. It will create a profoundly rich culture that is specific to your family, and it will affect your generations to come. Your children and your grandchildren will reap the benefits of the rock-solid, positive home environment that you will co-create.

CHAPTER TWELVE

PRINCIPLE ONE: LOVE AND RESPECT EACH OTHER UNCONDITIONALLY

Communicate! Communicate! And communicate! That is the key to keeping a marriage going in the right direction. It's communication that can convey your feelings of love, respect, and care, which actions sometimes mess up. Keep a check on your actions, as they speak louder than words.

Start out your marriage discussing the acceptable code of behavior. For all married couples, the first and foremost rule is to love and respect each other unconditionally all the time. Making a marriage work is a **conscious choice**. So unconsciously, do not slip into a mode that can derail you.

Recently, I came across an Indian couple, Raj and Bubbly. I used to see them quite often in social gatherings; unfortunately, now they are separated. They were married for twenty-three years with two children. Bubbly comes across as a polite, caring, bright, and beautiful woman in her late forties. She seems very cautious and reserved most of the time. Raj comes across as a bright and handsome young man who cares about family and family values. Though he seems hung up on the lineage of his family. They are both professionals and make a decent living.

From Raj's conversations it is clear that he is desperate to get his family back. His son and daughter also moved with their mother even though they are both in college away from home. Raj talks about them so fondly and about his wife so desperately. On one Sunday, Raj met my husband in a nearby shopping center. My husband invited him to join us for a cup of tea. He accepted. This is what he shared about his separation:

"Bubbly is a nice person. I have no problem with her. Whatever I say, she doesn't talk back. It is her mother and her siblings who are a wrong influence on her. As soon as I leave home, they all start calling my wife. I told her that I don't want any contact with that family, but she doesn't listen. It makes me crazy. When I question her about it, she just zips her lips—absolutely no comment—and that drives me insane. She visits them without telling me. How do I know? I note the mileage on her car. Sometimes she comes up with a story that she went to such—and such department store to return something. I know that particular article had not come from the store she claims. How do I know that? I check the bills to see which location a particular purchase came from."

This account clearly revealed that he loved his wife very much. For whatever reason, he hated her family. From his conversations with us on many other aspects and scenarios of his life, I came to know that

Raj has a bad temper. He is abusive in his language. He constantly puts down his family. He has severe control issues. He puts his parents' family on a very high pedestal and assures himself that nobody else is as high class as he is. In other words, he is full of himself. His wife and children did not match with his mask (ego).

He always disrespected his wife and her parents' family. His wife's family was in India for the longest time. Since they immigrated to the USA, Bubbly wanted their involvement in her life. Raj wanted her to be totally cut off from her family, and she did not want to do it. After a long struggle enduring such a stressful relationship, she quietly moved out.

It appears that Bubbly had never communicated to Raj successfully that her family was very important to her—or at least it did not get through to him. Why would you deprive your wife of a loving relationship with her mother and her loving family? Why would she give up that relationship if that is the only relationship where she can actually comfortably communicate; where she feels safe talking; where she is loved and accepted?

**Loving each other unconditionally means
respecting each other's wishes too. If you cannot
deal with your partner's family, at least do not take
away your partner's right to interact with them.**

You've got to trust your partner.

**You cannot be watching like a hawk every move
your partner makes.**

Here I am referring to the tone of communication, the language used, the emotion involved, and the impact of all that on the life span of a marriage. Both partners must consciously agree to uphold this rule.

One of the barriers to great communication is the belief that communication is nothing more than talking and listening. However, learning how to really understand your partner, as well as learning how to genuinely express yourself, involves a lot more than simply talking and listening.

**The first step in communication is recognizing that
we don't have to have someone to blame.**

It's not necessary to pass judgment to get your needs met.

We don't have to point finger at anyone, least of all our spouse.

When you begin this process, it's a good idea to ask your partner to explain to you what, exactly, he or she is not happy with in your marriage. Be open to the answers you are given, listen to them carefully, and pay attention to how you feel as you receive this information.

It is understandable if at first you feel hurt and want to defend yourself and possibly even put the blame back on your partner. But this will accomplish nothing as the point of this exercise is not to assign blame, but rather the point is to make your marriage stronger, more open, and in the end, to improve the intimacy in your marriage.

Approaching your partner with anger will only work to drive a deeper wedge between you and your spouse.

When you find yourself feeling angry, resentful, or just hurt about an issue that your spouse is trying to share with you, it's important that before you respond, you stop and take a deep, calming breath. Remind yourself that you are not perfect either, that you have made mistakes, and take a moment to think of things you can change with your own behavior as you move into the future.

Sticking with Raj and Bubbly's story, suppose that Raj shares with his wife that he is jealous of the time she spends with her parents. Bubbly may instinctively want to make her spouse see how much it means to her to see them. Maybe he is just feeling neglected. Bubbly should know that her spouse probably already understand her reasons. What matters is that she understands how Raj is feeling. This is where the negotiations begin, and real communication starts to take place. Genuine conversations build trust.

It's important to approach any of the problems your spouse shares with you with the attitude that there is always a satisfying resolution to the problem. Working to find a resolution to a problem can lead you to a place where there is more than merely talking occurring.

You can begin to really communicate, and with that the intimacy for married couples starts to improve almost immediately. But first you must abandon the blame game and the put-downs and put your focus on finding solutions to the problems. Once you can make that shift from blame and mistrust to loving, honoring, and respecting, you will be able to find solutions that will be satisfying and enjoyable for both of you.

When the other person is keenly listening to you, you feel respected. You find the body language of the other person positive and leaning towards you. You find that they ask questions or air their opinions believ- ing that you will contribute positively to the dialogue. In such a situation you feel respected and involved. Your self-esteem gets a boost, and you respect the other person in turn.

Is respect always a two-way street? Disrespect sure is a two-way street. You may be trying to respect the opinion of the other party, but the other party may be so disoriented due to anger, frustration, or other reasons that he or she may simply brush aside all your opinions and argue with you with total disrespect. How do you feel? Can you still respect that person, especially if it is your life partner that you are dealing with?

Regina and Tom got married after a courtship of two years. They were searching for a home to purchase and were referred to me by a common friend. I noted that Regina was a very verbal, candid, and assertive type of person. Tom, on the other hand, did not say much and did not question much; he trusted his wife's knowledge and wisdom in the field of house hunting and financing. During the time of courtship, Regina had visited Tom's family home and met his parents, grandparents, and siblings. Regina did not like anything about Tom's family, including the way they lived and the way they talked, as if they were from a different planet. Regina made no apologies for talking down about her in-laws.

She openly ridiculed them in front of her sphere of friends. Tom appeared to justify his family. If Tom made a remark, she stopped him before he could complete his sentence. Each time Tom rolled his eyes and stopped. He would not look up for a while. I could see from his body language that he was hurt and embarrassed. Regina was unaware of his reaction.

Tom was a hard-working man, never loud, never demanding. He was good-looking and earned a good salary. He never asked for much. He quietly but grudgingly agreed with his wife.

I told Regina not to test the limits of this patient man. She replied, "He doesn't care what I say. He will be fine." Four years later Tom packed up and left. They are now divorced.

How can couples meet one another's emotional needs better? How can couples prevent emotional infidelities from happening in their marriage?

When two people become bonded through marriage, they depend on one another for their emotional needs getting met.

But what happens later on down the road? Let's take a look.

When a spouse expresses their opinions, thoughts, and ideas and the other spouse invalidates those feelings, a spouse can feel rejected and unneeded. You can keep the fires burning in your marriage by agreeing and supporting one another. Marriage should not be "her way" or "his way" but "both your way"—teamwork. Most marriages have the husband doing his own thing, and he has his own friends and hobbies, and the wife does her own things and has her own friends and hobbies. They are pulling away from each other rather than working to be together and applying teamwork in the marriage.

In marriage, the husband has his roles and responsibilities that should be attended to and the wife has hers. Together they make a team because they complement each other's position in the marriage.

But when the wife tries to overthrow her husband's manly protection and position in the marriage, the balance of the marriage becomes upset. It works the other way too. Couples should be working with and encouraging each other so as to complement each other's position in the marriage. Couples lose interest in each other and think they are not in love anymore. Couples desperately need to be encouraging and supportive with the person they married.

When emotional needs don't get met, we tend to carry around a negative attitude about the person we married. Faults and weaknesses of our spouse become magnified.

We may clam up and think bad of the person we married, or we may become angered and say mean things to our spouse—or worse, become violent.

When a spouse feels unloved, rejected, or dismissed because of the lack of intimacy and spiritual oneness in the marriage; couples go outside the bounds of the marriage to get those needs fulfilled.

But this does not work. Let me tell you why. This behavior will hurt your marriage. Simple flirtations also involve emotions. In search of an extra marital thrill, you can get involved with the other person. This will give you temporary and superficial happiness but will sabotage your marriage. Is that what you want?

Communication is the key to any relationship. If you don't talk, you'll struggle to assure your spouse. People believe that if there is something in your heart, then it'll come out through your mouth.

If you really care, say you do. Talk about things. Work out your differences. Talk. It is words backed up with our actions that bring the most security to someone else. One without the other just fosters doubt.

Never say, "I do not need you." A marriage is about needing one another. It is about being greater than the sum of our parts. To not need your spouse is a problem. But more than simply needing each other—none should learn to say it out loud.

Men have a need to be admired as one would admire a hero. Women need to be admired as one would admire beauty or something very precious. Maybe you haven't figured it out by now, ladies, but your husband has an ego. He loves it when you stroke that ego. He loves to be thought of as capable and strong, the knight in shining armor if you will.

And women need their husbands to admire their beauty, personality, and general presence. Men like that too, and women sometimes like to be admired for their capability as well. But in all cases, it is clear—we need our spouse to admire us.

Everyone likes to know that their efforts are appreciated. When someone does something for you, say thank you. Don't take what your wife does or your husband does for granted. Gratitude and appreciation go a long way to strengthen any marriage.

Every husband has hurt his wife. Every wife has hurt her husband. Learn to say, "I'm sorry." Not in a flippant, arrogant manner, but with sincerity and honesty. There are too few apologies in marriages. Mostly, when we mess up or hurt someone we don't apologize, we just pretend it didn't happen. But that sends the wrong message.

When you don't apologize, you indicate that you don't care. Trust me, that's not a message you want to send unless you want more conflict. Even if you don't feel that you were in the wrong, apologizing for your part in the problem will go a long way.

If a couple feels stuck in a tug of war, this is what they should do. Take a time out. Put your emotions, comments, judgments, and your ego on hold and at rest so that one can objectively understand what the other person is trying to say. If needed, apologize and mean it sincerely. We mess up frequently. So practice forgiveness. Apologies and forgiveness propel you forward; it puts you back on track.

Loving and respecting each other means:

- No nagging
- No controlling
- Saying simply and clearly what you mean, meaning no satiric remarks
- Speaking politely
- Absolutely no harsh language at any time, no matter what
- Make a suggestion, not a decree
- No negative remarks about your spouse's family. Accept them for who they are; after all, they are integral part of your other-half.

CHAPTER THIRTEEN

PRINCIPLE TWO: DON'T BE A HARD-LINER

Let me continue with Raj and Bubbly's story. A very compatible couple with two beautiful children, now ages twenty-three and twenty-one—at least so I thought. After the wife packed up and moved out to an undisclosed location and the children decided to join her, Raj shared the sad news of his family abandoning him. My husband again offered to have a cup of tea at our place. Raj accepted.

He seemed like a wounded lion. His ego was the only thing that was still sticking out. He looked as if life had been sucked out of him. Upon my probing, this is the gist of what he shared.

"I love my wife very much. I cannot imagine living without her. The children went with her because she does not question their whereabouts. The children are on her side because I don't want them to be out after ten p.m.; I don't want them to be on the phone after ten p.m. I want them to have breakfast on Saturday and Sunday morning at eight a.m., but they are always late. It is my job to teach them the right things in life. When I lecture them, each time, it falls on deaf ears. . ."

Raj destroyed his family because he is a hard-liner. He thinks that he is the man of the house; his word should be the word from God. He gets no input from his wife or children. He talks at them.

People keep only those promises that they make, where they have a shared vision of responsibility, of obligation, of fulfillment.

When you set rules, make it a joint venture of all the parties involved. You must have input from your partner. Make sure that you two are on the same page. If you tune out your partner, you start to derail your marriage.

Actually, the impact of being a hard-liner reaches far beyond your marital relationship.
You are carving the path of your future children and grandchildren. The life that they will experience with you— their mom and dad, will shape their lives ahead of them.

So don't let them be confined to experiences that they will remember with awe and disbelief.

Choose your guiding rules in a manner that your partner feels part of the decision making process and what's right for both of you. Do not deprive your partner of the opportunity to have a say; your partner should feel at home—loved, believed, and trusted. Instead of taking things away, provide a warm and welcoming environment so that your partner can relax and feel safe. This process will help him/her to break away gradually from the past and on to the new family unit which is stronger and safer.

Do not let your family crash on to your hard lines so badly that you are unable to collect the pieces and put them together to move on.

CHAPTER FOURTEEN

PRINCIPLE THREE: COMPROMISE IS A VIRTUE

What is a compromise? Isn't it giving up something? Why should you give up something that you want or like? How can that make you happy? These are the questions that pop up when you think about compromise.

Marriage is a wonderful and beautiful thing, but it takes patience, time, and a lot of compromise. There are thousands of marriages that end in divorce because one or both parties did not want to accommodate the other. They feel that they have an obligation to fulfill, so they will marry their partner. They don't realize the scope of what marriage means.

When you take your marriage vows, you are promising each other that you will live by them. Living by your marriage vows on a daily basis will help keep your marriage strong and full of love.

To have that dedication and love for one another is a sacrament. No, I'm not saying that all marriages are roses and chocolates. Every healthy marriage has its arguments. Their disagreements lead to understanding each other's viewpoint. Don't get discouraged when you have a fight. Think of it as a learning experience and move on from there. Happy marriages are not built overnight, but through time and along with the effort you put into it. As with anything else, the more effort and hard work you put into it, you will see great results. Remember when you are getting married, or if you are already married, to live each day by your vows. Your marriage will be healthy, strong, and filled with all the love you want. It takes compromise, hard work, and effort to make a happy marriage, but it is worth it. Nothing will compare to the love you have for your spouse. But with that thought, when you have a happy marriage, a happy family will come out of it in the end.

When you are in a relationship, it's not about you alone; it is about you two—a team.

Be willing to give up for the good of the team, for the benefit of the team, for the peace of the team, for the harmonious growth of the team.

It is about tolerating the other person and his/ her mess— physical, emotional, and social.

To clarify this point, let's take a look at a scenario. Suppose that you have lived alone in your gorgeous one-bedroom apartment. You know exactly where your things go—it may be in piles on the floor, or neatly tucked away in an orderly manner. The bed might be left unmade in the morning—it's yours, and it does not bother you.

When you take a roommate, who happens to be your partner in love, immediately, you have to give up or share space—this is compromise. Suddenly his pile of clothes is in the way and it bothers you. It's the first symptom. Be prepared to give up some of your ways and start adapting to some of his/her ways. Or perhaps you are a vegetarian, and your partner craves meat. You both will experiment with each other's choices and meet somewhat halfway. That is partnership. That's how compromise is a virtue. Don't be threatened by it. **Social Accommodations**: Let's say for example that you have a habit of staying out late on Friday and Saturday nights, and on Monday and Wednesday, you go bowling with your friends.

How do you make time for your partner? How about your partner's schedule? Now your partner is the prime focus, not your friends. Your friends might make some cutting remarks for not showing up for social events. It should not bother you. Now both of you have to work out how much time you should have together. Friends who are really important to you will understand.

For you to get the best out of your relationship, you need to make time to be with your partner. Some people make the mistake of spending most of their time on their work, business, or even social functions. Unless it's really crucial and it's a job requirement that you must spend extra time there, don't do it just as an escape from the one you are married to. If you are staying away for the wrong reasons, catch yourself. You are taking a risk. You are drifting away.

It also translates that you are giving your partner the impression that he or she is not as important to you as your other commitment that is taking most of your time. Your partner will believe that you do not love him or her from the bottom of your heart, because if you do, love has a very strong attractive power. Where there is true love, there is always the desire to be with your partner. If you make the mistake of not devoting time with your partner, then your relationship may be heading to the point of collapsing.

Here is another reason to be with your partner: lacking your presence can create room for a foreign body to come into your relationship and tear it apart. For example, if your partner is lonely and another person offers to come around and keep your partner company, the closeness between your partner and that person can spark off love feelings between the two of them. No matter the nature of your work, business, or other commitments, you should always devote a reasonable amount of time to be with your partner. Your being together puts life into the relationship. Your closeness increases the love feelings for each other. You have the time to play together and share your thoughts and ideas on so many issues. You will have the time to plan your lives and plan for the future. It gives you the opportunity to study and understand each other very well so as to build a strong and happy love relationship.

Suppose that you grew up in a big family, and possibly you are very close to your family—your parents and siblings. They have to communicate with you frequently and vice versa; you depend on their viewpoint even on small issues.

Also suppose that your partner is a loner; no one in the family from his side is interrupting in any shape or form. Your partner does not like your connection with your family. Respecting your partner's perspective, you will make your contact with your family in a less visible manner.

You will also make your partner see your perspective—that this is how it has been all your life and you desire to continue with this close relationship because it is good for you and it makes you happy.

Your family will have to win over your partner or at least make him/her feel comfortable when they are around. Your partner should not feel threatened by your family's presence; instead, highlight the benefits of your family being around and available should any of you need help. Benefits always make the sale.

Emotional Compromise: Let's say you are a person who loves to show affection anywhere, even in public places. You love to take your partner's hand and take a walk in the park. Your partner is totally against the show off affection in public. You both need to compromise. You should talk about how you both can feel satisfied with mutual understanding and respecting each other's viewpoint.

We are social creatures.

We crave both physical and emotional contact with other people, and we will often do whatever it takes to have that contact.

So whenever you're not feeling close to your spouse; you can easily find yourself looking to someone else for that closeness; and that brings a real danger to your marriage.

When there is distance among a couple, particularly emotional distance, there is always a chance for things to go wrong. The longer this distance goes on between you and your spouse, the more difficult it becomes to heal.

Make sure that you fully involve yourself in what your spouse is interested in, and make time for you both to be together. Talk to your spouse regularly and share moments of love just like you did when you were courting.

When things go wrong, if you and your spouse can't talk about it, then you have a tough job ahead.

Here is another scenario. Suppose you are the one good at solving problems. You brainstorm about issues and come up with a most suitable solution. On the other hand, your partner cannot sift through all the emotional baggage he/she is carrying around. If there is any issue, your partner winds up being a wreck, with no clear thoughts, lots of stress, and whining. In this case, you should take on the role that you are good at. Let your partner not take the toll of issues that you can handle with simplicity and ease. It is a give and take, making space for each other, case by case.

When my husband and I came to the USA, our son Lally was only five months old. I got pregnant with a second child. My husband was highly accomplished in his field—he has a PhD in astronomical physics. He had better earning potential at that time.

I had a strong desire to become an economist. I got evaluation of my educational courses and found out that I had a long way to go. We both did not want to raise our children with babysitters or nannies. So I looked into options that could give me an opportunity to learn something new and make a career out of it without sacrificing my time with my growing family.

I chose a real estate career. I had to spend very little time to get my real estate license. It turned out to be a career that is flexible as well as financially and emotionally rewarding to me. I worked part-time while our boys were in school. As they left home for college, I jumped into a full-blown real estate brokerage career.

Our boys are very accomplished, balanced young men. I do not feel any less of me as I had to sacrifice my desire to be an economist. Do I have any regrets today? No. My compromise was for the common good of our family.

Looking outside the box, we always have options for positive solutions. As a married couple, you need to pick the options that serve you best as one unit. As long as you both see the benefit in making compromise for the good of your partnership, it is healthy. It is rewarding.

**In marriage, compromise is not giving up;
it is making room for growth.**

CHAPTER FIFTEEN

PRINCIPLE FOUR: DON'T TRY TO CHANGE ONE ANOTHER

Loving our spouse is giving them the freedom to be who it is they are and have been. When we are asking the person to change, we are imposing conditions. Once married, we must accept our spouse for being who they are, faults and all.

Couples waste so much of their time and energy trying to change each other to make them match their own ego. But is that really what needs to be done? The answer is no. It cannot be accomplished. Why? Consider the following:

We are the product of our past environment. It's irrelevant if it is good or bad, it's what it is. Like a little seed sown into the earth, it flourishes into a full-blown plant based on its soil and how much nurturing it got from the gardener. Ironically, better yet, unlike the seed, a little human with the power of its consciousness can change the way it blooms out as a full-fledged person and carries the ability to change still, if it wants to. The gardener in this analogy is our total environment. Bear in mind that habits are deep rooted. They don't just go away. The bearer has to consciously allow any change. So no one wants to change, simply, because that's what they learned growing up, and it worked for them then; it's you who has a problem with it.

Habits are not a costume that you quickly can change into.

Really, we just need to try and not let those little things bother us. Even some of the bigger things we can detach from. Communicate about the issue. Let your spouse know what bothers you, but don't make it into a tirade. How about a little bit of acceptance! It works wonders.

Once we focus on acceptance, our mind immediately stops the flow of negative feelings. It suddenly shifts gears.

When you are out of the criticism mode and you are in the acceptance arena, then find an appropriate time and have your spouse's permission to discuss what part of his/her behavior bothers you. Tell them how it affects you. Most of the time, your partner has no idea that he/she is doing something that's irritable to you.

I learned my lesson the hard way. My sons were about two and four years of age. I was a stay-at-home mom. We lived in a two-level townhome. We had off-white furniture in the living room and almost white carpet. So it was prone to easy staining. I had to put in a lot of effort to keep the house clean.

Every weekend, Malkiat would relax by putting his feet up on the coffee table with the newspaper all around him. The boys used to have their toys all over the floor with their father. They seemed to have a blast of a time, while I was miserable. The scene of clutter all around in the living room was very troublesome for me.

I must have yelled at my husband and the boys many times for making such a mess. I recall one day my husband said to me very nicely, "It's our home. We should be able to scratch where it itches; we should be relaxed the way we best can. Why are you so bothered with the clutter? If we are going to have company, we will clean it up."

Guess what? My perspective changed. Instead of getting angry, I joined them and did my own things. After the end of relaxation time, we all pitched in and cleaned up. They were all happy. I was not so miserable. Possibly, the kids would learn some messy habits. Possibly, I would have to have the sofa and carpets cleaned more often, and so forth. There was no other common area where my family could just "be." But they were all together and happy. After that incident, I started to evaluate each and every situation with a question—what's the worst that can happen? What is the highest cost I might have to endure?

These questions put things in the proper perspective.

Making a marriage work is a conscious choice!

If your partner has some annoying habits, don't be a nagger. Provide alternative solutions. Stop criticizing and stop making put-downs. What it does to your relationship has far-reaching affects. Each time you scold or put down your spouse, it will shatter their confidence and make them angry; their love and respect for you will start to chip away, piece by piece. Some spouses start to seek time away from the spouse, away from the nagging. That will surely cause you to drift apart. Allow your spouse the freedom to just be. Accept your spouse! Love! Love is *created* by a person; so does hatred. Both do not just exist on its' own. They both take action and response to accomplish. Then it creates a cycle. It can be a cycle of love or cynicism which creates hatred.

The value of the love we give to our spouse is based on how we are feeling at any given moment and time. If we feel resentment or bitterness towards those we love, we'll inevitably love with resentment and bitterness, which is one way we place nasty conditions on our love.

We don't have to listen to those feelings of bitterness.

Whatever we are thinking, it comes out in our actions. Loving someone in the real sense of the word is allowing him or her to be who it is they are.

When we learn to accept, bitterness disappears from our behavior.

We think that if we could change our spouse, we'll suddenly be happy and contented with our self and with our spouse. We try and change our spouse because we have stopped accepting them for who they are. Therefore, we cannot seem to love them either.

With no love left to give to our spouse, we might think we have nothing in common anymore. Who knows, maybe we begin to think we married the wrong person. Suppose the person we met last week at work seems better than our spouse? Pretty soon we have brainwashed our self into believing our thoughts that turn into feelings sooner or later.

No wonder more than half of all marriages end in divorce!

We need to accept that and move on with our life; that moving on includes our spouse.

The give-and-take process is a natural occurrence; it is instinctive to do something nice for our spouse because they have done something nice for us. We give and take all day long with most of our interactions in our daily lives; it's part of life.

Most marriages work in this fashion; it is a good way for marriage to flourish and grow. It keeps couples on their toes as far as remembering to give of themselves periodically to their spouse even when they don't want to. This act culminates in love.

Now, there is a big difference when we put ultimatums on the table. Dishing out ultimatums is more of a nasty conditional love and is based on selfish thinking and usually stems from one or both spouses harboring resentment. "I'll love you, but only if you will stop going out with your friends." or "I will love you only if you lose weight," etc.

This is not love, but a selfish person trying to get their way through manipulation and ultimatums!

Most marriages can be salvaged. We have to stop thinking we can change our spouse. We really just need to try a little bit harder. It can make a big impact on your marriage if you let go of those things that you can't do anything about and stop feeling resentful. This is how to not change your spouse.

Acceptance is love!

We should also remember that men and women are wired differently. Men and women both know this, yet they continue to use the same, ineffective tactics to try to get to each other. So just what are those differences, and how do they affect the way that men and women communicate?

While men are more results-oriented and prefer a more straightforward approach with the easiest route to the end, women operate in a different manner. Women tend to communicate in a manner that is conducive to and focused on building and salvaging relationships.

Now, when you are trying to determine just how this information will help you communicate better with women, consider this: If you talk to a woman in her language, on her level, don't you think that you will get better results than you would if you just forged ahead doing your own thing? Of course you would!

Women are also more inclined to talk things out than a man would. Women want to resolve conflicts, or perceived conflicts, by discussing various aspects of the situation. They want to rehash the topic over and over until it has been worked over and wrung dry of useful information.

Men, on the other hand, tend to clam up, preferring to refrain from discussing the issue, or they say their piece and then move on. This is what causes problems between men and women because the man shuts down and the woman feels neglected.

The smart man will take the time to listen to the woman in his life. He should not only listen, but respond to what she says. Ask questions, insert comments, and create some open dialogue. This will not only fulfill the woman's need to communicate, but it will also get issues out in the open and on the table so that they can be dealt with and faced. This could work to your advantage, particularly if you are in a relationship that you value.

Have you ever realized that once you got married, your tolerance towards your spouse's flaws dropped drastically? When in courtship mode, you are trying to ignore or overlook some of the stuff so that you can focus on what you really want from that relationship.

Why, after marriage, do we expect everything to be just perfect, exactly the way we like it to be? Couples come to realize that their partners, being human, also have flaws that normal humans have.

There is a saying that marriage is not ruined because of a third party. The marriage is already going downhill, and that is when the third party comes in.

As we become complacent in our roles, our expectations of each other get elevated over the years.

We easily get grumpy when the hidden expectations of our spouse are not met.

This is a trap. At this stage third parties become so much more attractive.

So let's see what we can do not to take our spouses for granted.

Don't expect your spouse to evolve into someone else after marriage. Remember, it is because you love that person, and that's why both of you got married. If you don't expect yourself to change, don't expect your spouse to change either.

Lay out your expectations for your spouse. Identify which are the unrealistic ones and strike them off. For example, if you expect your spouse to be more caring towards you and she is already doing her best, it is unrealistic to push her limits. If you want to have more care from her, show her more care first.

Couples love to play mind games. Talk it out verbally. Don't expect your spouse to be psychic and read your mind. Appreciate your spouse for being willing to change even a little bit for you.

People do not change because someone asks them to; they change when they want to, and when they give themselves permission to change.

Once you get married, accept each other for who you really are. Do not think that you can eliminate or change the part of your partner that you don't like.

Before you got married, you had your best foot forward. You were on your best behavior, hiding all the shortcomings that you were aware of. So many different areas of personalities surface when you start living together and which you were not aware of before. You may not appreciate what you see, but know that trying to change that in your partner is asking for hos- tility. Hold your tongue and adapt to it.

Do not get trapped if some family members expect something different from your spouse and you get sucked into the idea. You need to protect your spouse and uphold her/his right to be who they are and how they are. Do not start comparing the qualities of your friend's spouse with yours. Do not open that can of worms. Your spouse does not have to compete with anybody.

Remember that nobody is perfect. You may have your own flaws that your partner may not be appreciative of. Just focus on the positives and the cute stuff that attracted you in the first place.

If there are some habits that are irritating to you and you must discuss them, then do it in the privacy of your home and put it plainly and without any put-downs. Let your partner know how that particular habit is affecting you. Make a simple and timely mention and leave it alone. Your partner will try to change as long as he believes that will help the partnership.

Old habits die hard. Some of the stuff may be genetic that may take more than a lifetime to correct. Show understanding and acceptance. Remember not to sweat over little stuff. Ask yourself if any of that is worth losing peace in the family.

Do what is expected of you as husband and wife. Do not get carried away by whatever lifestyle your relatives or friends adopt. Do not get fooled as the saying goes—the grass is always greener on the other side.

CHAPTER SIXTEEN

PRINCIPLE FIVE: DON'T COMPETE WITH EACH OTHER

When you compete with your partner, you are in adversarial roles. When a couple is sitting in opposing camps, two things happen. First, one spouse will win and the other one will lose. Secondly, it will affect morale—the spirit of the spouses.

Much more than that, the balance of your wheels will shift. If that is the general environment of the home, there will never be creativity to propel you both in a positive direction. Both of you will seek opportunities to wrestle each other down. Love and mutual respect will never harbor in your abode. Synergy will never rock your cradle. Is that how you want to spend your lives, in a tug of war?

"Win-lose" is a syndrome of a control freak spouse. You walk all over the partner and make him/her feel worthless. "Lose-win" is a condition when one of the mates ends up on the receiving end, a martyr, a doormat. The minute you accept either of the syndrome, there is a chance of possible abuse. There is a chance of one of the partners feeling worthless. Both situations are bad for a marriage. Both spouses have to be winners to keep a healthy relationship.

Our society thrives on a forced ranking system—in school, at work, in sports, in our social environment. In this competitive world, home can be the only shelter where everyone can be number one—parents, children, and everyone else in the family. Relationships end up failing because they become victims of "win-lose" or "lose-win" attitudes, among other reasons.

There has to be balance, equilibrium between a husband and wife where both are equal, both believe in each other and both respect each other. They are always willing to let go of their ego for the common good of the relationship. Both partners stop being single at heart and become married at heart. They care more about the health of the relationship than they do about winning an argument.

If one loses in a battle of egos, the other one does not win either.

They just drift further apart.

**As long as you battle for power or control,
you are both losing in your marriage.**

Be aware of your personality. Are you a loner? To maintain the health of marriage means giving up the loner's behavior consciously and slowly. Marriage imposes serious responsibilities upon an individual, so a loner cannot survive in marriage. Marriage requires the opposite of independence—interdependence. If you think that you have too big of an ego that knows no submission to or acceptance of the existence of other individuals' rights and liberties, then your marriage will fail miserably.

Let's go back to the story of Raj and Bubbly. Raj put many restrictions on Bubbly. She could not talk to her parental family. She was not supposed to visit them. She tried to hide her activities from Raj. When Raj found out, he scolded Bubbly. Raj wanted his word to be the rule everyone must go by. His winning was more important than anything else. Even though Bubbly did not talk back to him, she lost all respect and love for him little by little. Back in the fifties and sixties, when women did not work outside of home, men were the sole breadwinners; a lot of marriages turned into abusive relationships. People did not divorce that frequently back then, but now times have changed. Most couples are dual-income families. So the new generation bears responsibility to build relationships which are creative and proactive, thus creating a culture of mutual trust, mutual respect, and understanding. The health of the relationship is much more important than silly little games of "me" and "mine."

If you start out right and move from "I" to a "we" unit, you can avoid a lot of unnecessary pitfalls of conventional marriages. Both of you will yield to what is best for the family. When you flourish with that decision, you place a high value to "synergy" and mutual respect for each other. Your family culture will harness a profound value system that will give your next generation a rock to hold on to.

❖━━━━━◆━━━━━❖

CHAPTER SEVENTEEN

PRINCIPLE SIX: UNDERSTAND YOUR PARTNER'S PERSPECTIVE

Have you ever stared at a full moon on a starry night? How do you interpret the shadows in the moon? Ask a group of buddies to join you in this adventure. To make it more meaningful, bring friends from diverse ethnic backgrounds. Go to an open space and just lie there and describe what the dark spots in the yellow moon look like to each one of you.

As a child, I remember my grandma used to describe the scene in the shadow of the moon. She made me see an old woman spinning a charkha (a wheel-like tool to make thread from raw cotton) and a man cultivating a farm with two bulls and a large hoe. Then she would say that when people die, their spirits leave the earth and go to the moon. So she would talk about all her dead relatives and look for them in the dark spots of the moon. That was my old grandmother's world of perception. Even though I know of the moon quite differently than my grandmother did, I still recognize shadows the way she described it.

We see the world through our own pair of glasses or the way we were conditioned to. Our own background, our own value system, our own experiences lead the way to interpret a scenario; the truth might be far removed from our reality. In order to understand someone else—their actions and reactions, their assumptions and expectations, we must see the situation through their lenses. We must step out of our own reality; we must put away our own pair of glasses.

How can we love and respect each other truly if we don't understand each other's worlds? Our relationship can be superficially respectful if we can focus on loving someone unconditionally. It can be functional. We can make the relationship work artificially. But in order to build a relationship at a level where synergy can take place, where we can influence each other without using status or force, we must understand the other's perspective at a much deeper level.

As a couple, you two come from different households, maybe from different cultures or a different socioeconomic environment. Falling in love or initial attraction is a matter of the emotional connection.

The pain you experience in your relationship originates when you realize that you are totally misunderstood.

If both partners experience the same and nobody tries to dig deeper to understand the other's world, then the relationship starts to drift apart. Assumptions and false expectations take over and work their way up. Before you know it, you recoil in your own skin. You strive for survival. You build a defense system just to exist.

In order to be in a nurturing relationship as a married couple, you need to understand each other's world in its original colors.

When you first start to get to know each other, when you are in fascination mode, it is a great time to listen to each other's stories. You have not yet developed expectations. You will not judge as yet—just listen and absorb. Once life happens, you become judge and jury.

Why understand the other person first? To gain an edge on creating synergy, you will be more effective while coming up with ideas to accommodate your partner in your life. You will be magical. You will be able to create an environment where your partner feels accepted, appreciated, and understood. If both of you have a mindset to understand the other first, imagine the positive energy that will fill your home and your hearts.

We all wear social masks. We have expectations of ourselves that may be a bit farfetched. If someone else confronts us with reality, we feel busted. We deny that reality. Our ego stands in the way. Our pride keeps us there. That's where ugly moments of door-slamming and put-downs erupt. Your world gets shattered. A bad cycle of rejection and anger can linger on.

After I read Stephen Covey's *7 Habits of Highly Effective Families*, I was constantly confronting situations where I needed to understand my husband's world first. Here is a glimpse of an incident that spoiled seven days of my vacation in England. How? By not understanding each other's perspective.

Back in 2005, the two of us were on vacation in England and France. My aunt lived in Leicester, England, with her family. Her children are a lot younger than me, but I have fond memories of my cousins as they visited my family's home in India every two years or so. It was a fun time playing games, going to movies, and making frequent stops at the college canteen for delicious snacks. Even more than that, I remembered how my aunt used to give me a bath and play with my curly hair and then sprinkle talcum powder on my body before dressing me. I smelled good. She appeared so proud. Why? I didn't know. I was the first and only little girl in the family. I must have been four or five years old at that time. My aunt was not married then. She was the number three sibling in my mother's family. My mother was number two.

When we were planning on going to England and France, I did not bring up the subject of possibly visiting my aunt who lived in England. Knowing that my husband does not have much connection with his relatives,

I thought he would be bored if I asked to visit my aunt for an evening or so. Therefore I kept quiet.

When we were in the hotel in London, I started to look at the map to spot where my aunt was residing before setting out for the first day in the streets of London.

"Let's go," he said.

"Just a minute," I said and kept searching the map with my glasses on.

He came closer and said to me, "What are you doing taking so long? We are getting late."

"I am trying to see where aunt Pritam lives. Maybe we can see her too while we are here in England," I answered. My husband took a nasty tone and whispered, coming closer to me, "I am not going to waste my vacation on seeing some relatives that I don't know and you have not met for the last twenty years."

My world was ripped apart. All the memories of childhood that gave me goose bumps for quite a few days were ripped out of my chest. I was not unreasonable to put undue pressure on my husband if their location was not convenient to visit. I did not bring up the subject again. I tried to enjoy our holidays. But deep down, I was suffering from an internal bruise that my husband was not aware of. I realized that it was partially my fault. I had not prepared him for a possible visit to my aunt when we were planning for our vacation. He did not know what fond memories I had of my aunt and her children. Because he was not close to any of his relatives, he could not fully understand and appreciate what it could have meant for me. He probably did not know how hurt I was.

From here on my antennas were up to understand his world, his perspective first before I proposed anything. After twenty-five years of marriage, I found out (finally) what ticks him off. I don't think he wanted to hurt my feelings. He just could not afford to add another agenda on a very loaded day. I get it.

His essential nature requires him to know in advance what we are going to do—be it for the day or the near future. Unless something of extreme importance comes up, then I would press my point. I would not be angry or hurt. I would just explain the urgency. I know that he would agree without any resistance. I am the spontaneous one; he is very structured. I get it now.

Did he have the right to overrule just like that what was so important to me? Did he have the right to hurt me? I think not. But if I am stuck with the thought that he had no right to hurt me, I could still be very angry and hurt. I did not have to compete with him if he was right or wrong. Only one of us had to recognize what had caused that moment of flared temper. I am glad that I did. The knowledge of his essential nature that he must know beforehand makes me forgive him and move on.

Now I bring up the issues that I like to accomplish way in advance—be it an expense or planning of a party or just planning of a day. I explain to my husband why I feel the need to do what I am proposing and how the experience will benefit me/us; I have no problem getting things done. He is genuinely helpful, he is part of the decision, and we are genuinely excited and happy.

When my husband wants to do something, he shares it with me. I dig out why it is important to him. We plan together and achieve double the pleasure. Synergy is at work all the time.

Start from the very beginning to freely let each other in on your respective worlds; it will do a whole lot of good to both of you.

**You will be part of each other's small and large goals.
You will be part of each other's joys and sorrows.**

**You will avoid the path to bitter arguments,
anger, and resentments.**

**You will give your children a culture of a very
healthy caring, loving and a happy family.**

In hindsight, when I first got married, the first year was very hard. I was excited to be involved with my husband's family and his world. I came in with certain expectations—my expectations based on what I thought "should be." My disappointment was that his world did not resemble my expectations. I was disturbed and disappointed.

My attitude mirrored how I was feeling—pretty low. Here I was wrapped up in my own struggle to fit in and be accepted. It was not happening. I was miserable. I wasn't mad at anybody else but my husband. He could see through my attitude and did not try to find out what was bothering me.

He probably was wrapped up in his struggle to match me up with his family's expectations. It wasn't happening either. I tried to share my side of the world—the environment in which I grew up. I had mostly happy memories. I loved to talk about silly stuff that kids growing up do. I was trying to share with him my perspective of expectations and so forth. I was trying to have him understand my perspective first.

Every time I tried to narrate my world to him, he reacted and gave me the cold shoulder. Soon I found out that he had no interest in knowing my world. It actually annoyed him. I was heartbroken. A deep pain existed in my heart. I wasn't aware that I was judgmental.

My husband accused me many times of feeling superior to him. That was not the case at all. However, for him that was the reality. When I would ask him about his childhood experiences, he would not open up. He had branded me. Every time I spoke of my childhood happy experiences with my siblings, I felt that my husband had receded into another layer of his protected territory. My pain got deeper. I was totally unaware of his pain that I was solely responsible for.

Life happened; we survived with the sheer focus of our commitment to our marriage and to our children.

My pain existed throughout. I knew we could reach another level of understanding. My husband seemed content. I think he had adapted his expectations, or that's what they were to begin with.

So far as I was concerned, I was constantly aspiring to be a better individual. I read self-help books endlessly. On my husband's fiftieth birthday, a good friend gave him Stephen Covey's book The 7 Habits of Highly Effective People and a couple more. I read the books with great enthusiasm. Floodgates of new knowledge opened and consumed me. I found myself guilty as charged (by my husband).

I cannot change the past. But I can make good use of this knowledge now. I already know his world just by being around him and his family for more than thirty years. Now I know how to approach his vulnerability. Now I respect every fiber of his being. I respect him and his family genuinely. He still does not understand the importance of indulging in other people's life stories. But I do. I listen emphatically. Our sons automatically do this— listen emphatically and without judgment.

Most of us go in circles playing judge and jury without knowing why. This role causes families to drift apart. Be aware.

Be an emphatic listener. Volunteer to understand your partner first.

Once you know your partner's world, you will be very successful in achieving true happiness in marital bliss.

CHAPTER EIGHTEEN

PRINCIPLE SEVEN: NEVER GIVE UP ON NEGOTIATION

Communication is the key to all negotiations. Positive energy gets to work while we are in negotiation mode. The minute we give up hope, all positive juices stop flowing. Stagnation takes place. Relationships shut down. This is one thing that we cannot afford in the pursuit of a happy union. Negotiation must stay at work. *Marie worked with my friend Pam as a property manager at a large rental complex and became a good friend with her. Marie did not have any family or friends in the area. Doug and Marie were married for seventeen years with two children. They had a terrible marriage. They never understood how and why they were together; but they were.*

Doug was a nervous wreck most of the time. If his job was under a threat of a layoff, he would start worrying and whining before it actually happened. If a child spilled something, he would go on and on yelling at the children and Marie and would not let go of the issue. If everything was going well at home and work, he would worry that something was about to go wrong sooner or later. You guessed it right—never a stable and peaceful moment with Doug.

Their growing children were usually sad and upset when grouchy Doug was around. They would often say to their mom, "Why did you marry this idiot?"

Marie was usually calm in her demeanor. She did not seem to appreciate anything about Doug. Marie came from a stable home. Perhaps she wanted to give stability to this marriage at all costs.

Marie would usually let out her frustrations just by talking it out at work. But a couple of years ago, Doug was laid off from work for four months. Staying home all day, he made it unbearable for the mother and children. He was loud, nasty, and upset all the time. He became hysterical. Marie found it very difficult to deal with him.

Marie tried to shut him out. She started to sleep in the children's room. At work, she was disturbed, tired, and depressed. One month passed, and the situation did not improve at home.

She opened up to Pam and said, "I don't know if I can take this any longer. I think I have to leave him." Then Marie did not show up for work for a week. She called in sick.

She did not leave him. In a rage, Doug had slapped Marie's face for not talking to him. She then threatened him that she would leave him. Doug's jaw dropped. He was speechless for a minute. He roamed around. Then with tears in his eyes he said, "I knew that. You are just like my mother."

"What the hell you mean by that?" said Marie. "When I was growing up, my mom and dad always fought. My mother had walked out on me and my dad, many a times. She would go for weeks and then return home. I was always afraid that I might not see my mom ever again. But she always did. But you don't fight with me. Now you are not even talking to me. I can't handle that." Floodgates of new information had opened. Now Marie understood that his fear stemmed from his childhood insecurities. Doug's mother fought all the time. She left her family for weeks or months. But she always came back. He felt very insecure with Marie when she stopped communicating with him and slept in a different room.

Marie saw a little insecure boy in Doug.

She did not leave Doug. Her reasoning was that "he is what he is." He did not drink. He was not cheating on her. He worked hard. He was the father to her children. She just focused on some positive streaks of Doug. They were not many; but just enough to hold on to her marriage.

Walking out does not guarantee happiness for Marie and the children. Now Marie has a handy weapon. She understands that Doug needs to be countered. Her silence puts herself in a deeper rage and it annoys Doug. She shouts back at him and then lets it go. I think Doug gets it. He is sure that he will not lose Marie and the children. He has now calmed down a bit.

Doug is still Doug. Marie is not a happy camper. But she isn't sad either. She still has to deal with Doug's nasty nature. But she deals with it with a smile. He thinks a world of himself. He cannot understand why anybody would have a problem with him. Their marriage, for Marie, is now tolerable; it's transactional at best.

No matter how difficult the situation is, no matter how exhausted you are, never walk away from the table calling it quits. Always look for alternatives to divorce. As long as you talk to each other, something good can come out of every situation.

To deflate any bad situation, remember to bear in mind the following:

Never use information that was shared with you in confidence. If you do so, your partner will not be able to confide in you any longer. He/she will feel manipulated and deceived. It will cause the two of you to drift apart. When we are angry, we babble without really knowing and approving of what we say. Our anger brings out the worst in us.

Words once spoken that are hurtful to the other, leave wounds so deep that time does not erase them.

Once we hit that rock bottom of hurt and pain, those words of hurt and insult surface time after time for years with the same force.

It feels as if you are pricking an old wound with needles. No matter how bad the situation may be, never use harsh words.

If you are arguing, do not walk out in anguish and close the door. The person you walk out on would feel very insulted, as if you don't care about what the other person has to say. The best thing to do in a situation where one person is lashing out, you should just listen quietly without countering. If you start defending your position, it's falling on deaf ears anyway.

Tell your spouse, "I didn't know this is how you feel. This was not my intention. I want you to calm down and we will talk about this later today (or whatever time you mean to talk about it)."

And do get back to your partner at that specified time. Make good on your promise. Talk about the issue, and both of you need to see it from each other's perspective. Apologize if you have done wrong. Your conversation will flow again. You will have feelings of love and trust.

If you take the approach of lashing back at your angry partner, you would say something to each other that would leave a deep scar in your memory. Not good. Make a better choice.

Prepare to navigate through some rough spots in life. You will encounter rough and tough situations if you stay together long enough in your journey. If you end up insulting and putting down each other, you are preparing for a breakdown.

When people get tired of daily fights and put-downs, they choose the easy option of calling it quits. From the get-go, learn to avoid making bad situations worse.

Always focus on each other's strengths and positives, no matter how angry you might be with your spouse.

After all, there was some connection that you two made when you decided to marry each other. You should focus on that connection.

If your marriage was arranged without you two knowing each other, then it is even more important that you always look at the big picture. Whenever you find yourself angry and frustrated with your spouse, detach yourself from the situation. You should take a deep breath and calm yourself down. You should recognize the source of your union and gather strength from it.

Infatuation withers and excitement cools off as you start to live together. You see each other in all moods; you see each other with disheveled hair and pimpled skin that you never saw before. Once you get comfortable with each other, it's okay to scratch where it itches. In other words, life becomes a bit tepid and a little less exciting.

That's normal. Accept it!

PART FOUR

GETTING BACK ON TRACK

Whatever common or uncommon grounds brought you together in a matrimonial union, you are there in it and you better keep it together. The majority of misery in marriage is concocted in our imagination. By amplifying everything, we just hear noise and confusion. Take a step back. Sort out your entangled web. Separate the issues from the fiction your mind got entangled in. Issues can be resolved. They will be resolved if you two commit to it.

CHAPTER NINETEEN

KEEPING A BALANCE

Whether you just joined the institute of marriage or you are thinking about it, or you are someone with years' worth of investment in marriage and going crazy and now disillusioned, you are reading this book because you want to keep it together. Or are you looking for a confirmation of your belief? Whatever the reason may be, you want to succeed in your mission. Whatever common or uncommon grounds brought you together in a matrimonial union, you are there in it and you better keep it together.

You need to keep your marriage tight at all stages of life. You need to depend on each other for physical, moral, emotional, and all kinds of support. A rift is easy to develop and it will grow if couples are not careful. Some couples who have had a very structured life tend to relax in their positions and don't think about their spouse too much. They assume that it worked for so long, so we don't need to do anything differently. If that was the case, then why do well-functioning marriages go downhill after twenty, thirty, or even forty years?

When couples come to a point when their marriage is functioning on autopilot, there is nothing much to worry about. Perhaps the kids are growing up or already grown and gone, and the wife and husband are each doing their own things. When you don't need each other's input that much, life becomes dull. When intimacy drops below the tepid point, it is time to be concerned about your relationship.

**Why many couples fall apart at the midlife
point or in their later years?**

A vacuum sucks the life out of their relationship.

Do not ever allow vacuum to set in.

**Stay interested in each other. Never lose
intimacy. Intimacy is not just sexual.**

It is also an emotional bond. Couples need to stay mindful of it.

Couples need to stay interested and dependent on each other. When people start to spend time separately and take separate vacations, their energy and focus get diverted. They develop new interests. They find more excitement with their newfound projects and relationships and thus begin to drift in different directions. And they mistakenly believe that there was nothing left in their marriage, that there was no love left to share.

Wrong! Wrong! Wrong!

**Love is still there. You just don't know
how to ignite passion anymore.**

**Love lies in little actions of kindness and care which will create
a chain reaction of loving kindness, which in turn, will work
as a catalyst to ignite the passion that has been in sleep mode.**

**If you rush into finding a new partner, after a
little while, that relationship will also lose its
steam and excitement too; and then what?**

We have developed a culture where we are always looking for excitement. That's all fine and dandy, but the result is devastating to the institution of marriage at large. The commitment to a lifelong contract is violated. How did we as a society stoop this low?

We need to raise our social consciousness and realize that we are headed in a wrong direction—we have not only failed in keeping up our commitment to marriage, but we have let down our children. We have denied them the opportunity to believe in and honor their commitments. We have let down our society. We have created a chaos in social order. The element of "honor" is losing its steam.

Marriage is a contract for life; it takes both spouses to stay loyal and committed to see it through. Interdependence, not independence is the core of a great marriage. A loving relationship is giving without asking, giving even when you feel you can't give.

Love is that lava that you just have to allow to erupt. It's always there beneath the surface.

However, we humans are imperfect beings by design. Even with the best behavior, we all are subject to disappointing our partners sometimes.

Misunderstandings and expectations borne out of entitlements, little jealousies, little power struggles— all of these things can cause a lot of turmoil in the home front. Little things can hurt the gentle breeze of paradise you two are trying to create if you do not guard it with your hearts and brains.

It takes 100+ percent commitment from both partners to succeed in marriage. Commitment of 99.9 percent though very close is still short of 100 percent; it's capable of turning things upside down. The little gap left by .1 percent can be deadly. It can grow out of proportion and tumble a rocking marriage.

When a couple is committed to pull through under all circumstances, they will.

Understand that our relationships evolve depending upon our performance in the daily humdrum of life. When you actually love and admire someone, you consciously or unconsciously ignore the shortcomings of that person. If that person responds to your emotions in the same way as you do, then love perpetuates and flourishes. You have a rhythm going on.

Does this mean that there should be no trouble in the paradise you two create together?

Wrong, wrong, wrong!

Life happens.

Circumstances beyond your control take over your life.

You must see those situations objectively.

Some things just spin out of proportion and create turmoil.

**You need to understand how to rock your cradle to
balance when it is spinning out of balance.**

If you feel that you can't take it anymore, if you feel that you are at the verge of calling it quits, then read on. In the following chapters, I am writing about the most common stumbling blocks that threaten most marriages. You will find tips on how to untangle your specific situation and come out ahead.

CHAPTER TWENTY

ASSUMPTIONS AND MISUNDERSTANDINGS

Assumptions and misunderstandings are viruses of the mind. Once planted in your head, it will create sufficient data to support its rightful existence. Then it will continuously look for new evidences to confirm its position. With repetition, it will become your belief. Early on in your relationship, when you want to believe that you know your spouse like the back of your hand, you may be up for surprises. It takes years and years of living together, going through ups and downs together that a couple can clearly understand each other.

Every day consists of our behavior in performing small acts that come from our gut of loving and accepting someone unconditionally.

One can argue that love is conditional except for love of parents toward children. Yes, I agree one hundred percent. We have to make a conscious effort to ignore things that make you not love your spouse. The dangling carrot is the destination of sticking it out all the way to the end.

Marriages that fail don't give the opportunity to get there where one has the luxury to figure the other out completely. Those couples drop the ball mid-field.

**Give no room to assumptions for it will lead to misunderstandings.
Communicate! Communicate!
Communicate!**

It does not take much to bruise a relationship that could otherwise be near perfect. Simple and silly little acts can lead to disaster if you are not paying attention.

For instance, let's go back to Judy and Kenny's story from chapter five. Both of them really loved each other, but they didn't say it out loud. Because of Kenny's father's death, the whole family was trying to cope with the tragedy. Judy felt like a fifth wheel. Kenny made no attempt to assure her of his love. Both of them did not nurture "we" as a unit. They were newlyweds.

Timing was very crucial for the growth of the two as a family unit. Judy showed no patience or empathy. Lack of commitment to "we as one unit" or "for better or worse" broke this marriage.

**Balancing Act:
Create a belief system:**

Create a belief system that suggests that two of you are together till death do you apart. Create a belief system that suggests that you trust each other, love each other, and respect each other. It does not matter how long you have been together. It does not matter that your experiences tell you something different. You can create a belief that you want to believe.

Repetition causes habits to form. Whether they are physical habits or a thought process, they tend to influence you. If you are looking for positive solutions, you will find resources to satisfy you. If you are a person infected with negative thoughts, you will produce a bundle of evidence to support your negative behavior. In any relationship, if you talk to two parties in dispute, both will have different versions of the same issue. The facts may be the same, but how they interpret the facts, makes all the difference. If we don't convey the other how we see the issue given the same facts, we are not communicating effectively. It is more common and more complex when two parties happen to be spouses.

Therefore all truths are half truths. This means that there is a 50 percent chance of a particular interpretation being true and 50 percent chance of being false. If there is a 50 percent chance of the same truth not being true, then why would you believe the 50 percent that impacts you negatively? Why not believe in the other 50 percent that will propel you forward to bring about the desired results?

I came to marriage with the belief that my husband loved me, he was the right compatible match for me, and I loved him. So nothing else mattered.

In the course of my early days of marriage, I was confronted with specific scenarios where assumptions and misunderstandings could have come between the two of us—assumptions that were creations of my own mind, not substantiated by any other data. We were both struggling to fit in each other's world; I was able to overlook and override the evidence that did not support my belief. His world was very different from what I had in mind.

However, my actions were taking place under this pretence that everything was okay, when it was not. The only source of strength was my faith in my husband and myself in loving each other. It propelled us further. My actions caused favorable reactions, and the same goes for my husband. Chain of actions creates a belief system. We both have impacted each other so much that now some people say that we are identical in behavior. Of course that is after spending time together day after day, year after year— believing in each other, respecting each other. We have adopted each other's philosophies of life that made sense to both of us. We have evolved as one unit.

You can too.

Never entertain the thought of walking away:

Once you entertain that thought, your actions start supporting that negative thought. You will forget all the positives that led you to marry the person in the first place. Know it for sure that entertaining the thought of leaving will lead to disaster.

Walking away also means that you are saying goodbye to negotiation. If you have a definite misunderstanding, give it a good chance for explanation. Try to understand from your spouse's perspective. If you walk away, you have everything to lose; what's the hurry anyway? You will do something revengeful or stupid and it will add to the baggage without resolving anything.

Stay intimate:

Show physical affection and emotional support. The person who has a misunderstanding usually shows the grievance in many ways. Your daily attitude bears the flag that things are not on an even keel. It's the responsibility of the partner possibly at fault who has to make the effort to get to the bottom of things.

Put all other issues on hold. Take a break from work. Make special arrangements to spend some quality time with each other. Be intimate. When you have found out the source of the issue, make sure that it doesn't happen again. If it does—and it will until you get to know each other on a deeper level—promise that you will communicate.

Don't criticize:

Don't criticize your partner's behavior that is making you uneasy and distant. Instead, tell him/her how it is affecting you and your relationship. Chances are that the person inflicting the pain on you is not even aware of the impact. Communicate. Have a dialogue, not an argument. Respect each other's position. Don't give up.

Renew your expectations:

As the air eases up, renew your expectations positively and fairly. Keep your expectations real as life happens, and each time a conflict arises, you will see a different side of your partner. You are sharpening your knowledge of each other's strengths and weaknesses. Understanding the weaknesses will prepare you to navigate the turbulent situations peacefully; the knowledge of your partner's strengths will boost your confidence and double your ammunition for your upcoming journey.

CHAPTER TWENTY-ONE

SURVIVING ANGER AND DISAGREEMENTS

No matter how sweet and polite you are in love, like all married couples, you will get into arguments over something over the long haul. As imperfect human beings that we all are, our desire is to show the other that he is wrong and you are right. Even though you probably know that you are not all right and your partner is not all wrong (unless there is a misunderstanding), imperfect human nature is to lure you into winning the contest.

Know that it is okay to argue; it is normal. It is also healthy in a marriage. But argue fairly and tactfully.

Know that it is an art to argue and deal with situations calmly, wisely, and successfully.

Also know that this skill can be acquired.

Actually, it takes a paradigm shift. Find out the underlying issues that caused the anger and then the argument. Is it that your partner failed in meeting your expectation in a certain situation? Is it that he/she did not acknowledge something that they should have? Is it bedroom performance that leads you to be angry?

If you understand the reason for your anger and disappointment, you need to find ways to express your point of view effectively. Anger closes the door to understanding. Anger denies you the right to be understood. How can you resolve a situation with your partner if you don't allow yourself to get to the root of the problem?

My good friend Jasmine has learned to live life with her argumentative husband, Govind. Govind's male ego is so big that he cannot bear to be wrong. If Jasmine argues with him, he quickly loses the battle and gets angrier. The situation has spiked to dangerous repercussions many a times.

Jasmine does not feel loved or respected. Even though Govind praises his wife to others all the time, he can never acknowledge it directly to her. The man does not drink alcohol or use drugs. He goes to work and comes home. He has no other bad habits that Jasmine complains about. He is a penny-pincher. Jasmine loves to enjoy living fairly well. He likes to control the money. He decides when to have guests for dinner (i.e., his extended family and friends), that too without consulting with his wife or lending her a helping hand.

Jasmine's stress level has gone through the roof. Her doctor has a very good relationship with her. She has communicated the root cause of her stress with him. Off and on, she has been on depression medication under her physician's supervision.

She has had thoughts of divorce. When she discussed those thoughts with me, we talked about if there would be a benefit of divorce to her, to her only son, her social life, and her finances. She is totally opposed to finding another relationship. It would raise her stress level to see her son hurt. She has a good relationship with his family, and she would lose all that. Billy, the only child, does not see his father as a bad person; he was leaving for college anyway. So leaving the marriage would mean even more stress for Jasmine. She reached a conclusion that it was not worth getting out of marriage.

So we talked about how to handle all the strife coming from her husband. This smart woman has done two things to deal with her situation. She separated her checking account. She explained to him that she has no hidden expenses of her own. Whatever money is spent, it's for the good of the household and the family. Having a separate account gives her the freedom to do all that she has been doing all along without his interference and thus unnecessary conflict.

This gave almost a heart attack to her husband. It took months before he stopped bringing up the account issue. But finally, he did. For Jasmine, more than half of her life's misery is over.

Secondly, she has learned never to let any argument escalate to a level where he has to feel defeated. She quickly diffuses the situation by not arguing back. When he is in the mood to argue, she hears it out and acknowledges, but does not feed into it. In a few days, she introduces her game plan on the same issue with a benefit package. He finds no grounds for disagreements. Even if he does not like something, he does not get angry. He offers his two cents, and she gladly honors it. This time his recommendation does not come of his ego point, which is always combative. It comes from a calm and progressive point, which is in compliance with positive solutions. Now Jasmine has eliminated most of the conflict from her daily life. I don't think Govind has changed one bit.

But their marriage is transactional at best.

This is achieved by understanding each other's true nature. If you understand what ticks off your partner, find a solution to bypass the situation. As long as both partners have the desire to stay in the marriage, they will. Just learn to deal with each other's vulnerability and the ship will move smoothly.

My husband Malkiat and I had very different priorities to use our funds. Soon we learned that both of us would have to give in. I recall arguing when shopping for furniture for our new home. Money was tight. I wanted the best furniture money could buy. So I had to visit a lot of places before agreeing on a piece of furniture.

After three or four episodes of getting angry and frustrated and returning home not talking to each other, we learned something new about each other. We established that while Malkiat is very good with allocation of money, I am very good with picking colors and styles that work well with our space.

We agreed that Malkiat would tell me what was the comfortable amount and the highest amount we could afford to spend. Keeping that in mind, I did my searching. When I arrived at the final selection point, I took my husband with me and showed him my narrowed-down list, and the decision was easy. Over the years we learned about each other's nature, habits, strengths, and weaknesses.

With a little understanding and with God's grace, since the boys got into their teenage years, we realized that they needed understanding and acceptance with love and respect. Malkiat and I stopped being traditional parents. Before we told them what was required of them to comply, we just introduced the issue. We asked for their input. We pitched in ours. The results we achieved were astounding. Nobody ever talked loudly or disrespectfully in our house. Our family of four has developed amazing respect toward each other. We all hear each other out and get to know the position each one is coming from. We brainstorm together, throwing all options in the pot. Amazingly, the ideas that seemed so distant and so wrong at the outset seem quite workable after the brain- storming session. This creates synergy and excitement and a peaceful rhythm.

How to Keep and Maintain Balance:

Remind yourself that you are not enemies; you both want a positive solution that benefits the whole family. Avoid going into win/lose or lose/win mode—it is pure poison. Keep yourself in check while in an argument. Do not turn your back and leave room while you are having an argument or even when you are talking at a high pitch. Walking away is giving up. It leaves your partner angrier. Just don't feed into that frenzy; remain calm. Do not acknowledge that you agree or disagree with it. Acknowledge that you understand what position he/she is coming from. Ask for more time to think through it. Once the situation passes and flared tempers have calmed down, you can have a fresh start on the subject.

Never use something that was confided in you at a previous time. If you do that, you break the trust in your relationship. It will make your partner feel emotionally unsafe in the relationship.

Understand that if you deal with each episode with respect and understanding, it will bring you both to a new point. This will be your new place, where you both have a better understanding of each other.

The attitude of positive solutions will bring about your individual strengths and weaknesses that you two can effectively use to nurture a healthy relationship.

CHAPTER TWENTY-TWO

DIFFUSING POWER STRUGGLES

As the time changed from the 1950s to 1970s, the concept of women's liberation suddenly changed the rules of the American family. In the fifties, it was all a one-income family system. Very rarely, women worked outside of home. This kept expectations of couples very clear. Husbands and wives had different duties, so there was hardly any clash. Husbands were the breadwinners, and wives did all that was needed to run a household. I am not saying there were no problems back then. There was power abuse. Men did whatever they wanted and got away with it. Women suffered and the children suffered.

When looking back at past eras, the 1950s is looked upon by some as an idyllic time in American history. The nuclear family headed by a male breadwinner was the desired norm, and televisions shows such as *Father Knows Best* and *I Love Lucy* were popular.

However, there was a dark underside during this era. Women were treated like second-class citizens, and some were living unhappily married because their financial and educational options were limited. Some women were forced out in the workforce during World War II. This caused a shift in family values and altered the family structure for future generations to come.

As we moved to the hippie generation, it was not all family-oriented. They did crazy stuff, which also led to the deterioration of the family. Women worked as well as men did. Some men had to share chores at home. Women's movements for liberation led to dual-income families. It was an era of confusion. Our family system broke down. Power struggles erupted. The male ego was bruised with wives being equal breadwinners. In today's society, women are competing with men in almost all areas of the socioeconomic environment; hence the power struggle is at the peak.

In the 1960s divorce became more socially acceptable. Among certain people, however, it was still not considered right, and it was still not common. As it became more acceptable, it inevitably became much more common. Eventually it got to the stage where anyone in an unhappy marriage would consider divorce, and this obviously led to much high divorce rates.

However, the fundamental truth about marriage still persists. The truth is that if a couple's relationship is based on love, trust, respect, and commitment to marriage, then nothing, and I mean nothing can shake it no matter whether we are talking about marriages of the fifties or the seventies or today.

Power struggles happen at all ages and stages of life. Women no longer feel that men are superior beings. Clashes erupt out of who is in charge of what. If the woman makes more money than her husband, it's a source of confusion for the man and woman both. Man's traditional position as breadwinner is threatened, and the woman now has access to all that an earning man had—more opportunities for better employment; resources to gain more knowledge; knowledge about changing the order of the society, changing rules and regulations that impact human rights; access to other men and women. And that enables people to cheat their partners in marriage.

Balancing Act

If we all adopt the marital code of behavior which I call the "Code for a Happy Ever After," there is no room for confusion. But I know, even if we are on our best behavior, we are only human. We fall off track. We don't know how to get back on in a timely fashion.

Adjust your paradigm of your role and your expectations in marriage. Pay attention to interdependence, not independence. Interdependence has a higher value than independence in marriage. Promote everything for "we" not "I." Think of marriage as a bank account. Let's call it a "we-pot." Whatever you create, endure, or struggle for should go into the "we-pot." You are depositing everything you own or wish to own into the "we-pot." You cannot claim individual deductions. Use the "we-pot" as a source of synergy.

If you start your marriage from this point, there is no power struggle.

If you have not created a "we-pot" so far, start it today, I mean now. If you want this marriage to work, you should have no hesitation to start your "we-pot" account. Not only do you deposit your income and all worldly valuables, you also deposit all your wisdom and knowledge; your strengths and weaknesses; your energy to give and receive emotional support; your love, respect, commitment, and trust. It doesn't matter how many accounts, stocks, or real estate, you individually own; as long as you think it is all meant for you and your spouse, you will be fine.

———◆———

In Hindu philosophy, two people in a marriage are equated to two wheels of a chariot. The wheels have to be perfectly balanced at all times; otherwise, the chariot will lose its balance and fall apart. It is the same in a marriage. If your marriage feels like a tug of war over every issue, you need to break that cycle.

Let your partner know that you respect what he/ she says, but suggest being open enough to explore some more options. Bring up your positive options. Be fair in judging. Nobody can always be wrong or always be right. If your partner is still right, acknowledge that. Have your opinion heard and weighed every time.

If you feel that your opinion did not count, let your partner know about it. If it got a fair shot, you gained some ground. Be aware of your strengths that are superior to your partner's. You cannot be strong in all fields of life. You should take responsibility for areas that you each are good with.

My husband has great skill in managing money and paying bills on time. I mess up every time if I have to handle this responsibility. Why would I bother with that responsibility? My husband manages our family income and expenses.

There are plenty of things I am good at. If something that I do bothers him, he plainly tells me, "Dear, this feels odd. Are you sure...?" This gives me a reason to rethink my decision, explore more options, ask for his input, and then reach a decision point. I do not feel put down or challenged. We are both moving in the same direction—the direction of positive resolutions.

CHAPTER TWENTY-THREE

SURVIVING FINANCIAL CHALLENGES

We all have financial challenges at some point in our lives. If financial challenges come coupled with many other stresses of life, it can blow your relationship apart. Debt and money problems are listed amongst the topmost issues that lead any married couple to file divorce. It is not actually the debt that is the main problem. Debt elimination can be handled with a proper budget plan and professional debt counseling. But instead of focusing their attention on the root cause and finding a solution, most couples argue over bills, spending, debt, and other financial issues.

Many times couples use credit cards for spending without keeping track of the amount spent by their partner and later feel overwhelmed by the total bill. The first thing they do afterwards is to blame each other.

Dealing with financial issues effectively therefore becomes more necessary if you are already in financial crisis. The way you choose to react to your debt will greatly determine whether your marriage will end or survive.

Here are some guidelines to dealing with financial problems while you are in a marital crisis.

Look for these three simple solutions:

Can you bring in more money to the table without sacrificing your time together? Even if you have to make the tough choice, make it as a temporary solution.

Can you cut down on spending? Look to all sources, not just his or just her spending. It doesn't matter who makes how much money. It is all yours', whatever is in your "we-pot."

Thirdly and most importantly, know that most marriages go through times of trouble. You must fight the issue on hand instead of fighting with your spouse. Focus on the problem, not pointing fingers.

Fighting and finger pointing will not resolve anything.

It will just deepen the hurt you two are inflicting upon each other.

You both must stand united. Whatever compromises you both must make, you should do so. Do not use the money issue as a reason to go separate way. Money problems are short lived or at least they can be handled. Do not let it challenge your marriage.

CHAPTER TWENTY-FOUR

SURVIVING EXTRAMARITAL AFFAIRS

When you are struggling in your own marriage, anyone who pays you a little attention looks very attractive. Suddenly that person becomes the prince or princess that you deserve to be with. Once you walk together as a married couple, suddenly you are awakened to the harsh reality that this newfound love is not fault free. Then you wonder how you could be so stupid to walk out of your first marriage.

When the wedding bells quiet, and when you start living as a husband and wife day in and day out and you fall into your comfort zone, married life becomes routine. You become you, without any conscious add-ons, and so does your partner. Life falls into a dull lapse unless you are consciously and contiguously charging it.

You don't always remember to say something sweet and nice or bring flowers to your partner. You see each other in your natural physical glory—maybe with pimples or skinny legs or disheveled hair in the morning—the imperfect beings that we all are. And suddenly it hits you that it's not the same romantic love anymore that once you had for your partner.

If someone else gives you a nice compliment, it draws you. It gets your attention and it feels great. A lot of people fall prey to this superficial feeling. People cheat to escape from reality. It happens in all age groups and in men and women alike. People dive into love affairs that start with simple flirtations—a huge mistake.

At all ages and all stages of life, there are times or incidents when you see people that you feel somewhat attracted to. That's a normal human experience. As a married individual, you should not read too much into that attraction. Consider it as a little disturbance in the environment. Do not focus on it.

However, if the attraction keeps catching your fancy and not going away, you need to shake it off. Remind yourself that focusing on that attraction constitutes a desire to cheat on your spouse. That will be a conscious choice that you will make. It does not simply happen. It will have repercussions that can be devastating to your marriage.

In May of 2010, Sean Hannity, a talk radio host, introduced a Web site that facilitated protection of identity to all who wanted to have illicit affairs by signing on to that site. Radio host Sean calls himself a man of family values and conservatism. Did he not feel a bit responsible for airing such an advertisement?

This trend is anti-family and anti-marriage. Most brain-dead people follow the trend. It does not mean there is a value to the trend. People who live their lives grounded in a superb value system who want to do right by their families and right by society do not become prey to these trends. People who care about family values will swim upstream to chase their convictions.

Before you act upon any temptation of having an affair, remember that the excitement induced will also be temporary and short-lived. Once you get to know that person, your thrill will die down. The longing to be with someone else is there as long as that person is unattainable. Once you have access to your newfound lover, all it takes is moving in together for the sizzle to be over. Why? Because that person is just another package—not the perfect human being that you were attracted to, but with all the faults and follies of a normal person.

According to a divorce lawyer, almost 66 percent of couples feel that they made a mistake by leaving their spouse for a love affair, that they would have been happier in their marriage. And if you have children involved in your marriage, the damage is exponential. Everybody loses materially (financially), emotionally, and spiritually. There is no peace; instead, all members of the family sift through the rubble of the mess left behind.

Before you take a step to enjoy the thrill of an extramarital relationship, think what is at stake. Think how many people you will hurt along the way for something that has very little chances of working out. Also think and process if it was your spouse who had an affair outside of marriage, how that would affect you.

Before you walk out on your spouse, know that you have the opportunity to recharge your marriage only by living it. Honor your spouse, honor your commitments to your marriage, and take the steps you need.

Can a marriage survive an affair? It all depends. It may appear to be a vague answer, but you have to understand that just as no marriage works on a textbook formula, the failure of a marriage also follows no fixed path.

Every marriage survives on a set of dynamics that are couple-specific.

An affair is usually the fallout of some gross interpersonal conflict which has become temporarily unsolvable.

Can a marriage survive an affair? The answer could be yes, if one goes by the past record of thousands of couples who have resolved the disputed areas in the marriage and have successfully moved on, living happily thereafter, so to speak.

However, there are also couples who could not come to any mutually agreeable solution to resolve the conflicts and have amicably parted ways.

Let us look at the problem in a positive light and find out how a marriage can survive an affair. The crux of the matter, most importantly, is whether the will to allow the marriage to survive is equally strong in both partners.

A third person enters the marriage way after the marriage is derailed. Look at the issues that caused the affair. It is not to blame the partner for not fulfilling all the marital needs, but to really look at what was missing in your marriage that led to the affair. If you can address the problem, then you can judge if the affair is forgivable and forgettable.

I talked to Ann, a good friend and a coworker who took her husband back after he had an affair for three long years. When she filled me in on the details, she candidly expressed that she was not going to give up on her love of thirty-five years. They shared children, they shared life with its most memorable events from the prom date with the same man to the birth of their children—their graduations, their weddings.

She admitted that the death of her long-time ailing mother caused her to stay away for months at a time. That's when George started a fling with a bowling partner who filled in when Ann was away. George was depressed with guilt until he came out and told Ann about it.

She also admitted that she no longer has the same trust in George. It hurt deeply even though she knew that the affair was over. She can't help bringing it up from time to time to give George a piece of her mind for putting her through the humiliation. She knew that wasn't right on her part. But that's how it is. She said that their marriage is functional at best.

She didn't know what else she could have done. At age sixty-two, she did not feel like starting over. What guarantee could she have from a future relationship that it would be hurt-proof?

There is your answer. She said it all.

Are you prepared to forgive your partner? This applies not only to the person who was involved in the affair but also the sufferer. Here are some tips to save the marriage even after it has suffered some indelible scars from an affair.

Any reconciliation or resolution of an interpersonal conflict is possible only through frank and accusation-free interactions.

Ideally, this should start as soon as you "feel" that there is an entry of a third person in your marriage.

Treat the affair as a wake-up call to sit up and do some disaster management to save a failing marriage. As mentioned, the first step is to start an open and frank dialogue with your spouse. If you do not listen to what your spouse has to say, you can never get the right answer to your question: can a marriage survive an affair?

Can a marriage survive an affair? Yes it can do so successfully if both of you are willing to forget the past and bring back the lost romance in your relationship. Forget about all other priorities and focus wholeheartedly on your spouse to save the relationship from any further damage. Spend as much time as possible with each other and give everything else a break.

Finally, remember an affair can cause an unforgettable trauma and putting your marriage back on track can take a lot of time, patience, and understanding. Of course, it also requires lots and lots of love and a common ground of desire to make it work.

Watch out—if you find yourself wanting to cheat, catch yourself. Be aware of disasters ahead. Be aware that each of your actions will have repercussions. Nothing goes unrewarded. Imagine how your behavior will impact the people around you—your spouse and your children—if you follow through with your little flirtation or affair. Your relationship with your family will change for good.

Imagine how you would react if your partner did this to you. If you give this issue a reality check and play it out in your head, the intention of cheating will leave you. You will regain full control of your commitment to your family. So nip it in the bud.

Analyze what is happening at home. Is it boredom? Or is there a real issue that your home front is not accounting for? Is it dissatisfying sex or just lack of appreciation for whatever you do? If it is sheer boredom, get busy with interesting and more rewarding activities. Help your partner in whatever way you positively can. Go volunteer your time. Boredom is in your mind. As your mind gets busy, boredom vanishes. If there is a problem at home, get to it. Work on resolving it. Ignoring it will not get you anywhere. Check your fundamentals of marital behavior. Find out the core issue and then resolve it by communication. Know that it is normal to fall into such lapses in life.

This is not the first or last time it will happen to you. Know that under every external façade, all couples have it, no matter what sweet talk they wrap it in. So know that you are not alone feeling flat.

Know that this temporary feeling of exhilaration born out of an extramarital relationship won't last long. Secrets don't remain secrets for long. It will end with guilt and depression ruining your relationship at home. It will bring you down.

Know that your new prince/princess charming is no different than what you already have. Once you get to know them, you will find that they are imperfect beings just like your partner.

Know that people who choose that path of cheating on their spouses are not happy individuals. Their lives become much more complicated, their laundry much dirtier, and their baggage much heavier.

Don't solicit advice from loved ones and friends. Most of the people will take your side just because you are their friend. Very few people will be truthful or helpful to you in making the right decision. People tend to keep up appearances. They will just agree with you. The fact is that you know what you are doing is fundamentally wrong. By talking to other people you are gathering support to further your selfish interest. Don't fan your fire. If you must talk to someone, talk to someone mature and maybe someone who has experience going on the same route and learned his lessons.

Recharge your marriage. Do things spontaneously. Do something extraordinary—take a weekend off with your spouse. Take a break from the daily rut. For a change, treat each other just like when you were dating—presenting your best self. Ignite and kindle all your positive memories of each other's beauty, of romance, of moments, and of places. You will experience a surge of new positive emotions.

Stay away from the person, the situations, and the places which fan the fire of wrongdoing. Do not share your feelings of flirtation or falling for someone else with your partner voluntarily. You may be thinking of getting it off your chest, not being aware how your partner will react to this trauma. Do not hurt your spouse if you can handle it yourself. What they don't know, they don't know.

If you catch your spouse flirting or cheating, do not hide the fact that you know about it. Instead, confront him/her right away. Tell your spouse that you are extremely angry and you want that nonsense to stop immediately.

Do not feel one bit guilty thinking you brought it on to yourself.

There is nothing you can do so wrong that allows your spouse to do something this low. It's your partner's doing of their own free will. Don't start blaming yourself and fall into a downward spiral.

Don't threaten to leave. Why would you want to give up something that belongs to you and your family—meaning your children? Fight for what is rightfully yours. Let your spouse feel guilty and embarrassed for something they should not have done in the first place. Give them a chance to explain the whys and the hows. You need to know everything so that you will know what to do in order to resolve the problem for now and for the future. Do not show any sympathy either. Support your partner in the endeavor to resist the temptation. Be there with your partner if the situation allows, especially if you suspect that the other person may be there. Do not make a public scene that might embarrass your partner. Do not fan the wrong fire. It will bite you back. Do acts that are viewed positively and that bring a positive resolution.

Let your partner, not you, put an end to the situation. Your partner needs to straighten up her/his commitments. Give her/him the time and opportunity to prove to you that all is back to normal.

Once the situation is resolved, do not bring up the subject again and again just to keep your partner down and feeling guilty. There is limit of punishment for every crime. If you keep your partner down low and treat him/her disrespectfully, you will be looking at a losing battle. Why? To have a balance in life, all parties have to feel healthy in the relationship. Feeling less than healthy will cause the weaker partner to resort to the same behavior to feel good.

Keep this a secret from your children. Never ever discuss it in front of them. If the incident happens later on in life when your kids are old enough and aware of what's going on, it's alright then. If that is the case, the relationship needs a major overhaul.

Remember that if you stick to your commitments of having a great married life, distractions and fascinations may catch your attention momentarily, but they will not amount to anything significant that your marriage should suffer.

CHAPTER TWENTY-FIVE

WORKING THROUGH SEXUAL PROBLEMS

I was amazed to watch a show on Oprah early this winter. The show was on this very topic. It had my full attention. Oprah brought on a middle-aged couple who had been married for more than thirty years who had sexual issues that they needed help with. They were sent to a sex therapist. The couple shared amazing results. This is the knowledge I gained from the show.

People are preconditioned about sex even before they actually indulge in physical intimacy. Men and women have predetermined ideas of their expectations of their partner's performance. Whether they read about it or learned it from home or school, their expectations might not be substantiated by factual knowledge, but some fixed ideas about sex are there. The couple that appeared on television was a normal, middle-class, conservative Caucasian couple in their mid fifties. The woman never had achieved an orgasm. The man was feeling guilty about his performance. They appeared very nervous and embarrassed.

Upon getting professional help, they found out that nothing was wrong with their bodies. The woman grew up with this notion that nice girls don't talk about sex. And nice girls let their husbands have their way with sex. So this woman had a tough time coming out of her shell. Her body was reacting totally opposite of her preconceived notions of sexuality when they were physically intimate. She had to train her mind to the idea that it is okay to feel sexual. It took a few weeks of therapy and guidance until the couple felt that they had full control over their sexuality. They were finally able to sort through their issues.

To my greatest amazement, I learned that 70 percent of women don't achieve sexual satisfaction for various reasons. And the good news is that they don't have to live with that condition and feel gloomy about it. It can seriously tar your relationship.

Behind every couple's divorce, there is some sort of dissatisfaction in the bedroom that is responsible at the core.

It may not directly be the reason for divorce, but most other problems in marriage germinate from it.

If you are not satisfied in the bedroom arena, talk to your partner about it. Luckily, there is help available for all kinds of sexual issues. Don't waste your precious days in misery.

Know that different stages of life have different dominant needs. As we grow old, sexual sizzle varies for men and for women. Do not feel entitled that if you can't get it home, you can have it elsewhere. Instead feel entitled to a great relationship at home, accepting all handicaps and exerting all resources for help.

Balancing Act:

Adjust your mysterious philosophy of sexual expectations. This is about your body, your sexuality; you have to be comfortable and satisfied with it. As partners in marriage, you have this one unique common field accessible only to you, husband and wife. You can have lunch with friends, you can share philosophies with other people, and engage in all kinds of debates, but your bedroom issues need to stay with you two. If there is any dissatisfaction there, you must openly talk about it. Come up with positive solutions. Seek professional help. It's all under your control. I am sure that there would be temptations outside of your marriage. Put a lid on that thought. Following your temptation is going to destroy you and your marriage.

Know that all couples need adjustments and tweaking in this field before they get it right. If you have issues, you are not alone. Also know that there is always hope for better performance, and you need to communicate about it.

Be understanding and respectful about each other's needs, desires, and fantasies. Do not ridicule your partner if you find issues with their likes and dislikes. If you do not fulfill each other's needs, there will be a growing emotion to get it elsewhere. So take care of each other.

If you find your sexual appetite to be much stronger or much weaker than your partner's, accept it. Seek medical help. Weak desire may be caused by some chemicals in the body. See a doctor and talk about the problem and your desired results—your goals in making your bedroom experience sizzle.

Raising children, taking care of an ailing member of the family, overwork, and stress can kill or suppress your desire for sex. If the condition is temporary, acknowledge it. Put yourself and your relationship before everybody else. There is nothing wrong with it.

It reminds me of the airplane rules. If the oxygen is low and you have to help put masks on your young children, you are required to secure your mask first.

Stay intimate. Take care of each other first so that you can meet other challenges of the daily grind of life effectively.

Frankly, guide each other by talking openly about your physical needs. Don't assume that he/she should know about it. Nobody is a mind reader. Many women complain about their partner not knowing the sexual mechanism of female anatomy. Let your spouse know about your likes and dislikes. Don't trust the thought— he/she should know. Men and women both need to be proactive. The results you achieve are for your mutual benefit.

CHAPTER TWENTY-SIX

SURVIVING ILLNESS OR DEATH OF A LOVED ONE

I met an amazing couple who was staying with a mutual friend in our social circle. The couple was uprooted for the second time in life. This time, they were victims of Katrina. They had left their home under extreme conditions like most other people did—they barely escaped Hurricane Katrina. Most people got into shelters. But this couple with two teenage children drove up north to stay with a childhood friend, Dave. Dave and Vicky called us (my husband and me) to have dinner with them on a Friday night. We accepted. We met the couple. Their teenage children were mentally challenged. They needed uninterrupted attention all the time.

We stayed there for two hours—and I mean a very long two hours. We were exhausted watching what went on. The teenage children, a boy and a girl, were only a year apart. They appeared physically normal and strong. Their son was about 180 pounds and five feet ten inches tall, and their daughter was about 160 pounds and five feet six inches tall, which seemed normal and healthy for that age.

They were both screaming and the boy was throwing things against the wall, against the floor, and sometimes up in the air. He shattered a few glasses in a matter of seconds. The boy was shaking uncontrollably, and their daughter was screaming at the top of her lungs—it was hard to watch. . I guess both kids hit the peak of their anxiety mode, and fits of uncontrollable anguish triggered with both of them while we were visiting.

Both parents hurried to take care of the situation. Both parents stayed with them for about ten minutes or so, and then we did not hear anything. They had moved upstairs to go to their sleeping quarters.

I was humbled by the faith and commitment the couple had for each other and their family unit. Without getting embarrassed, without getting upset, both parents hurried to control the situation. After the kids had calmed down, the parents joined us in the family room. They simply apologized gently. They made no excuses. They explained the status of their children's health. There were no regrets, no finger pointing, no discouragement. They simply said, "God gave us these children, and it's our solemn duty to take care of them." They both had jobs outside their home. They both worked less than full-time on split days so that one of the parents could be with the children.

In later conversations, we learned that what happened that evening was the norm. They apologized to the host and thanked them for understanding.

What resonated with me to this date is that the couple was at peace. All the statements they made reflected their positive attitude towards difficult situations. I noticed that there was love beyond measure and utmost resolve rooted in respect.

The moral of the story is that if you as a couple guard your relationship with deep love and resolve rooted in respect for each other, you can weather any storm. If you don't have a strong united front, the storm will break you. Many marriages break down when one of the partners give up and move away in difficult times.

Go into marriage with the awareness that there could be territories or situations you never thought even in your wildest dreams that you would have to endure.

Take life as it comes, with full commitment (Not 99.9 percent but 100+ percent) and undoubting resolve; life will yield to you.

**When your intentions are pure, and you stand
steadfast in pursuit of your joint vision of life;
trust that everything will be alright.**

If one of you has to take care of an ailing family member or an aging parent, the other spouse will have to be understanding. Remember to keep your focus on your family unit, and make sure that your family is knowledgeable about your whereabouts.

Make sure that your spouse does not feel ignored in your pursuit of helping others. Be away only when you cannot avoid it. Taking care of an ailing person can be very stressful for a caretaker. Make alternative arrangements so that you are able to catch a breath and be with your own family.

Too many times, we get so overwhelmed by the expectations and obligations of extended family. Do not be taken over by the obligations to a point that your spouse and family members suffer that they become unsympathetic and feel abandoned. You know your situation best and will have to balance both, but keep your priorities straight.

Death of a loved one is devastating and traumatizing. If your spouse looses a loved one, you need to pay extra attention to your devastated spouse. You need to show total emotional support for the loss. Lack of support can cause your partner to slip into depression. It's like being hit twice, with the second injury being more painful.

If you are anything like myself, this information about how serious marriage business is and how much you need to know before getting married, you could be overwhelmed to the point that you could become a skeptic. To marry or not to marry could be on your mind. I learned with great pain how to propel my marriage forward. The only thing that never changed throughout the course of thirty-three years of our marriage was the unshakable commitment to stick it out, no matter what.

Feelings of love and romance had withered away as life's brutalities trapped us off and on. But the good news is that love and romance came back as soon as the temporary insanity disappeared.

We have made a lot of mistakes. We suffered from them. We had hurt each other, but we were quick enough to catch our mistakes. Both of us came forward with genuine apologies.

Whether I brought income to the table or not, I was always my husband's equal. I respected that. His genuine love, respect, and care for me kept me grounded in the truth that we belonged together.

We are very different from each other. We were both fascinated with each other's personalities. We still are. We are very open and flexible. We both look at issues from untraditional angles. Maybe that is the biggest commonality we have.

I am very open with just about anybody who comes in contact with me. I am very trusting. My husband calls me naïve. He is a rather quiet but pleasant person. I do the talking sometimes even for him. I can come across as overbearing. But I do it just because my husband does not talk much. In my silly mind, I cover for him.

He is very brilliant, and I have an average IQ. I am socially very aware; he is closed up in that department.

I rely on his intellect to make tough decisions in life and my business. Sometimes he can be very petty; it annoys me. But I accept him because he is the product of his environment—it's not his fault. He is what he is, and I accept that. So I get over his silly little jealousies and pettiness.

When it came to raising two children, he left no stone unturned. I was a housewife for a long time. He took away the responsibility of handling the children and home when I was tired.

So many good things going! And yet we fought. Yet we hurt each other. We carried the burden of sponsoring our extended families from India. It put financial strain on us. It divided us. It united us. The bottom line is that we are still here — together; love each other with all our imperfections.

Our two children, Lally and Rajan, added to our life's joy beyond measure. They couldn't be what they are if they had to live through the insecurity of not knowing if their parents would be together or divorced. Some of our children's friends did not have the good fortune of having their biological parents together to see them grow up. Some of them got messed up and fell off track in high school. Some of them could not afford to go to college, living with a single parent. And they were equally bright kids. I feel for them.

Why did it matter to stick it out to the end, no matter what? Having or not having a rock-solid family—that is the ultimate option.

CHAPTER TWENTY-SEVEN

LAST BUT NOT LEAST

Life does not come by textbook rules. So no one can predict what is in store for you. If you are grounded in principles and you have mapped out your journey with a clear destination, you will find yourself looking at challenges from a totally different perspective. The challenges or the storms will not break you. You will find ways to navigate through them successfully.

So whatever situation you are in, no matter how complex, make adjustments and you will find yourself on the way to untangling your web. You have to have a clear vision and focus. Take responsibility for yourself. We always want our partner to change because we don't see ourselves objectively. You take the lead— to love, to apologize, to forgive, to forget and make amends.

Most problems originate from a clash in personality types. When the wedding sizzle cools off and when people get out of their put-ons, a person's true nature surfaces. No matter how compatible you are in all areas of life, still you are unique "you" and your partner is another unique one. How do you fit each other like a glove on a hand?

What are the options open when you find that you are bickering over little stuff all the time?

Walking away? No, that's not the option we are discussing.

Letting your partner have his/her way and you just exist there in nonexistence?

It is impossible unless you have a doormat personality. That would be the equivalent of slavery, not marriage.

Figure out if the clash is just a nuisance or if it is affecting one of you in a very big way. Here is a story of a couple who has been married for seventeen years. They hit rock-bottom and came very close to divorce. The wife suffered through depression and became suicidal. The husband kept gaining power and became verbally abusive until the wife stood up and pushed back. It's a case of a husband who had very low self-esteem and an ego bigger than his head.

This anonymous wife laid out the account like this:

"We got married in India in the traditional Indian way. We had no chance to get to know each other before we married. Here we were starting a life together. My husband is professionally educated, so he had no trouble getting a job. I did not work as we also started to have a family. I thought that was normal. The harsh reality of living with this man was that I was to live like a maid. I could not go shopping even for necessities. He did grocery shopping and all other shopping for our children. Nothing I did was right. I was not allowed to have friends or family over. I am a college graduate. I could pursue further education. But my husband would dismiss all my plans as if I was stupid to think of a job or education.

"I felt suffocated. I did not like my appearance. I began to feel that there was nothing I could do right. My body was aching all the time. I started to take a lot of over-the-counter painkillers. I felt worthless. I started to have thoughts of committing suicide.

"Then I decided to stand up. I found a job that offered training on the job. It was a commission-based job. After the first year, I was able to have good income-producing opportunities with a huge potential to double or triple my income. That empowered me. I stayed away from my family for the longest hours I could. Why? One reason, because I was working and producing. Secondly, I was happy. I had respect among my peers. I was no longer worthless. "My husband kept grumbling about my hours and still kept trying to knock me down with his cutting remarks. I did not respond to him, but I was smiling inside. Once I felt that my income was going to be stable, I opened a separate account. I told my husband that I would take up half of the bills. Things started to change drastically.

Now I could shop wherever I wanted to. I bought beautiful furnishings for the house. I was happy.

"I was able to do a lot more with my children. I started to make plans for family vacations. My husband did not object to my plans. My children were happy to be out having a good time with their mom and dad.

"It has been seven years since I got hold of my life. I don't think my husband has changed much. He is who he is—always negative, always complaining, always finding faults. But he does not get me down. My happiness stems from within me. My children are a great source of joy for me. They are getting to college age. I am pretty hopeful that they will do really well in their career paths.

"My life is rich. I have thought of divorcing him. But no! I will not do that. Life is bearable now. I will not rob my children of their father's presence. If I had no children, I probably would get away. I am pretty sure that I can make it on my own, financially. I look at the positives in this marriage. We are a functional family. Sometimes I just shake my head in despair; my husband gets the gesture now. He is milder in behavior now. Once in a while, he throws an ugly tantrum. I just dismiss it as no big deal.

"Believe it or not, he sometimes shows physical affection. It angered me at first. But I don't reject his advances. I am trying to give it back in return. That is just hard for me. My mind gets blocked by his previous perpetual behavior. I know I have to get out of this mode. Only then we can have a deeper connection; I don't know, maybe not."

Just as I discussed my friend Jasmine's story earlier, there are many other folks who have similar issues. When couples find each other bickering all the time even though there are no major issues, it becomes hard to tolerate each other day in and day out. Once you can pinpoint your partner's true nature, then it is quite possible to adjust the mechanics of the daily grind and make life livable.

We all deserve to have everything—a loving partner, lots of money, great health, wonderful parents and grandparents for our wonderful kids. Look around. How many people seemingly have a full package of all great blessings? Almost everyone is missing something that they would love to have. Explore the potential in your package and strive to make it better each day. Look for happiness in the realm of your domain, and you will find it somehow, somewhere. And that is my promise.

If you are looking to marry and to have a family, be diligent before actually committing. In this society and western culture, you have all the freedom and resources to meet and date people unlike some third-world cultures. Use your belief system as your guide in making a selection. Do it right the first time around. With a compatible spouse who you actually like and love to be around, you can embark upon a great long journey. Know deep in your gut that it is up to you how to manage your sail. Let the principles guide you for a happy ever after, and you and your spouse will be in charge. Life will bring challenges with some stormy weather; but nothing is strong enough to break your commitment to yourself and your spouse and to your purpose in life together. You will have a great journey but you are in control for it to be the best it can be.

It is important to understand and accept your spousal package. Accept your partner's limitations. No one is totally perfect; neither are you. Sometimes we are misguided and look at others' packages. It may feel that grass is greener, but that is from a distance. Instead, work on your own yard and make it a garden. Make it the best it can be.

Sometimes, we are miserable as we try to find happiness from the wrong sources. Don't hop from marriage to marriage in pursuit of happiness. You must take charge of your own life instead. You can generate that great rhythm that can be a symphony by itself. Happiness and contentment will find its way in. Peace will reside with you.

My husband and I have entered our senior years. In hindsight, life seems like a dream with delicious pain and tremendous joy. All the stupid problems we ever had now seem like silly stuff. When I revisit the problems I thought were deal breakers at that never ending moment, were actually projections of my own mind. My husband had contributed to them in some ambiguous way, but never with the intention that they could rise up to the level of deal breakers.

Exactly the same way, I revisit the moments of events when Malkiat felt I had deeply hurt him. Whenever that hurt surfaced to the ground which frequently did over the years, all I hear is how I made him feel at the moment. When we dig little deeper and sift through the actual conversation, his memory of it is quite different than what I had said or meant. I fail to understand how he could translate the conversation the way he did. One thing is for sure right, whether intended or unintended, either my manner or choice of words during those bitter conversations were such that it didn't matter how or what I said; I had hurt him.

The moral of this tale is that when you are angry or tense, you do not convey the message properly. Neither you nor your spouse has the clear ability to communicate effectively. In the heat of the moment, things are said and heard quite differently than intended. And couples start to take those statements to heart and can never know the underlying truth. In fear of another burst of emotional blame game, they try not to bring up that subject again.

See, the hurt is not erased. You pretend to go on in life as if the pain did not exist. Every time, another incidence takes place, new pain lays over the old one and so on and so forth. Your mind begins to believe that your spouse doesn't even care. And you two drift apart.

Do not go that path.

Had I known what I know now, or had I had access to the information that I do today, I could have saved tremendous heartaches in my married life. I was timid. I did not talk to anyone that I could trust would render good judgment. My own family, mom and dad, I never thought that they could understand what I needed in terms of great advice. For them, I was their brilliant daughter who deserved only the very best. They could have misguided me. I am glad that I never shared any of my life's little grumble with them. I am glad that I never doubted my love and commitment for my husband.

All of you, out there reading this book, here is my guarantee and promise to you.

If you start out right with a compatible partner who you love and adore before you get blessed by your priest; Be assured that you can have a very happy and fulfilling life together. Your love for each other, your commitment to uphold your vows, your daily behavior rooted in principles, following the Code of behavior I prescribe in this book, will see you through. You will make mistakes; and that is okay too. Frequently forgive each other. Trust your love. Don't give up on each other. There is something very sacred about your relationship; that's why you married each other; cherish that sanctity.

I have high hopes for our youth and upcoming generations. Baby boomers are at its exiting point of messing up the fabric of this society. The pendulum is already swinging to the other direction.

To procreate is our heritage. Same is true for animals. But we are different from all other species. By preserving good values, we progress as humans. Family provides a safe threshold to all potential genius in mankind. A strong, healthy marriage is the foundation needed for a strong threshold; conserve it, propel it. You will not only be happy in your own journey, you will be positively contributing to rectify the confusion in the human race of our times.

So go forth and take charge.